MW01641336

AMERICAN Better Living

FAMILY COOKBOOK

Editorial
US Food Editor: Linda Venturoni
Food Editor: Rachel Blackmore
Assistant Editor: Ella Martin
Editorial Assistant: Sheridan Packer
Editorial Coordinator: Margaret Kelly

Recipe Development
Jane Ash, Susan Bell, Belinda Clayton, Penny Cox, Sheryle Eastwood, Sue Geraghty, Joanne Glynn, Michelle Gorry, Donna Hay, Anneka Mitchell, Voula Mantzouridis, Meg Thorley

Credits: Recipes page 11, 14 by Lesley Mackley; page 94 by Louise Steele © Merehurst Limited

Photography
Andrew Elton, Paul Grater, Ashley Mackevicius, Harmo Mol, Yanto Noriento, Andrew Payne, Jon Stewart

Styling
Wendy Berecry, Rosemary De Santis, Carolyn Feinberg, Michelle Gorry, Donna Hay, Jacqui Hing, Anneka Mitchell, Anna Philips, Susie Smith

Design and Production
Manager: Sheridan Carter
Layout: Lulu Dougherty
Finished Art: Stephen Joseph

Published by
J.B. Fairfax Press Pty Limited

Formatted by J.B. Fairfax Press Pty Limited
Printed by Toppan Printing Co, Singapore

Some of the contents of this book have been previously published in other J.B. Fairfax Press publications.

JBFP 298 US
American Better Living Family Cookbook
Includes Index
ISBN 1 86343 137 3

Printed in Singapore

AMERICAN Better Living

FAMILY COOKBOOK

Contents

RECIPE COLLECTION

SOUPS

Whether it's a clear consommé or a hearty one-bowl chicken, meat or vegetable soup, nothing beats homemade soup. Leftovers are delicious for lunch – just heat and place in a thermos flask for taking to school or work.

Basil Meatball Soup, Pea and Ham Soup

Basil Meatball Soup

1 tablespoon olive oil
2 carrots, cut into thin strips
4 cups/1 liter beef stock
4 oz/125 g vermicelli
freshly ground black pepper

BASIL MEATBALLS
8 oz/250 g lean ground beef
1 egg, lightly beaten
3 tablespoons dry bread crumbs
2 tablespoons grated Parmesan cheese
1 tablespoon finely chopped fresh basil or 1 teaspoon dried basil
1 tablespoon tomato paste
3 cloves garlic, crushed
1 onion, finely chopped

1 To make meatballs, place beef, egg, bread crumbs, Parmesan cheese, basil, tomato paste, garlic and onion in a bowl and mix to combine. Using wet hands, roll mixture into small balls. Place meatballs on a plate lined with plastic wrap and refrigerate for 30 minutes.

2 Heat oil in a large skillet and cook meatballs for 10 minutes or until cooked through and browned on all sides. Add carrots and cook for 3 minutes longer.

3 Place stock in a large saucepan and bring to the boil. Add vermicelli and cook for 4-5 minutes or until vermicelli is tender. Add carrots and meatballs, season to taste with black pepper and cook for 4-5 minutes longer.

Serves 4

The meatballs for this soup are also delicious made with thyme, rosemary or parsley. Or you might like to try a mixture of herbs for something different.

Pea and Ham Soup

1 tablespoon/15 g butter
1 tablespoon olive oil
2 cloves garlic, crushed
1 onion, finely chopped
4 oz/125 g button mushrooms, sliced
4 cups/1 liter chicken stock
1/2 teaspoon paprika
3 stalks celery, chopped
10 large lettuce leaves, shredded
8 oz/250 g fresh or frozen peas
4 oz/125 g ham, diced
1/4 red pepper, finely chopped
2 tablespoons chopped fresh parsley
freshly ground black pepper

1 Heat butter and oil in a large saucepan and cook garlic, onion and mushrooms for 3 minutes. Stir in stock and paprika and bring to the boil, then reduce heat and simmer for 10 minutes.

2 Add celery, lettuce and peas and cook for 5 minutes longer or until peas are tender. Stir in ham, red pepper, parsley and black pepper to taste and cook for 3-4 minutes.

Serves 4

Serve this soup with broiled cheese triangles. Toast the required number of bread slices, cut into triangles and top with a slice of your favorite cheese and a few chopped fresh herbs. Cook under a preheated broiler for 3-4 minutes or until cheese melts and browns. A sharp Cheddar cheese, goat's cheese or Gruyère are all good choices.

Curried Lamb Soup

1 cup/185 g yellow split peas, washed
2 tablespoons vegetable oil
12 oz/375 g lamb shanks, cut in half
3 cloves garlic, crushed
1 onion, finely chopped
2 tablespoons curry powder
5 cups/1.2 liters boiling water
2 tablespoons chopped fresh mint
2 carrots, diced
2 stalks celery, sliced
1/2 cup/125 mL coconut milk
1 tablespoon lemon juice
freshly ground black pepper

1 Place split peas in a bowl, cover with water and set aside to soak for 10 minutes.

2 Heat oil in a large saucepan and cook lamb shanks for 5-6 minutes or until browned on all sides. Add garlic, onion and curry powder and cook, stirring, for 5 minutes longer. Drain peas and add peas and boiling water to pan. Bring soup to the boil, skimming off any scum from the surface, then reduce heat and simmer for 1 hour.

3 Remove shanks from soup and set aside to cool. Remove meat from bones and cut into even-sized pieces. Remove peas from soup and place in a food processor or blender and process until smooth. Return pea purée and meat to pan, then stir in mint and carrots and cook for 5 minutes. Add celery, coconut milk, lemon juice and black pepper to taste and cook over a medium heat without boiling for 3-5 minutes.

Serves 6

Economically, a hearty meat soup is a good choice, because usually a less tender and therefore less expensive cut of meat is used. A meat soup generally uses less meat than other dishes and so is a good choice for those trying to reduce their intake of red meat.

Veal Dumpling Soup

1/4 cup/1/2 stick/60 g butter
2 onions, chopped
4 slices bacon, chopped
1 lb/500 g lean veal, cut into thin strips
1/2 cup/60 g all-purpose flour, sifted
1 tablespoon paprika
8 cups/2 liters beef stock
2 red peppers, halved, roasted, skinned and chopped
1/4 cup/60 g tomato paste
1 tablespoon caraway seeds
freshly ground black pepper
2 tablespoons finely chopped fresh coriander or parsley

HERB DUMPLINGS

2 cups/250 g self-rising flour, sifted
1/4 cup/1/2 stick/60 g butter, cut into small pieces
2 eggs, lightly beaten
1/3 cup/90 mL milk
2 tablespoons chopped fresh herbs, such as parsley, coriander, rosemary or thyme

Serves 6

1 Melt butter in a large saucepan and cook onions and bacon over a medium heat for 4-5 minutes or until bacon is crisp. Using a slotted spoon remove onions and bacon from pan and drain on paper towels.

2 Add veal to pan in small batches and cook until brown on all sides. Remove from pan and drain on paper towels.

3 Combine flour and paprika, stir into pan and cook for 1 minute. Remove pan from heat and gradually blend in stock. Return onion mixture and meat to pan, bring to the boil, then reduce heat and simmer for 1 1/2 hours or until meat is tender. Add red peppers, tomato paste and caraway seeds and simmer for 15 minutes longer. Season to taste with black pepper.

4 To make dumplings, place flour and butter in a food processor and process until mixture resembles coarse bread crumbs. Place eggs, milk and herbs in a small bowl and mix to combine. With machine running, pour egg mixture into flour mixture and process to a smooth dough. Turn dough onto a lightly floured surface and knead quickly. Shape tablespoons of mixture into small balls and cook in boiling water in a large saucepan for 10-12 minutes or until they rise to the surface. Remove dumplings using a slotted spoon. To serve, place a few dumplings in each soup bowl, ladle soup over and sprinkle with coriander or parsley.

A hearty soup that is a meal in itself. You may wish to use beef in place of the veal.

To roast peppers, halve, romovo soods, placo them under a hot broiler (skin side up) and cook until the skin blisters and chars. Place in a paper or plastic bag and leave for 10 minutes or until cool enough to handle. The skins will then slip off.

Left: Curried Lamb Soup

Italian Chicken Soup

Italian Chicken Soup

12 cups/3 liters chicken stock
4 boneless chicken breast halves, skinned
1 teaspoon whole black peppercorns
4 bay leaves
1 sprig fresh rosemary
1 onion, chopped
1 red pepper, chopped
2 carrots, chopped
$1^1/4$ cups/185 g short pasta shapes, such as macaroni
8 oz/250 g cabbage, shredded
2 tablespoons grated Parmesan cheese

1 Place stock in a large saucepan and bring to the boil. Add chicken breasts, peppercorns, bay leaves and rosemary. Reduce heat, cover and simmer for 20 minutes or until chicken is just cooked.

2 Using a slotted spoon, remove chicken from pan and set aside to drain. Strain stock and return liquid to a clean saucepan. Add onion, red pepper, carrots and pasta to stock, cover, then bring to simmering and simmer for 20 minutes or until pasta is cooked and vegetables are tender.

3 Slice chicken. Stir chicken and cabbage into soup and cook for 5 minutes longer. Just prior to serving, stir in Parmesan cheese.

Serves 6

This clear chicken broth made with fresh chicken and vegetables makes a nutritious and delicious light meal that any weight watcher will love.

Spinach Soup

4 cups/1 liter chicken stock
$^{1}/_{3}$ cup/60 g small pasta shapes
8 oz/250 g frozen chopped spinach, thawed
freshly ground black pepper
2 egg yolks

1 Place stock in a large saucepan and bring to the boil. Add pasta and spinach and cook, stirring occasionally, for 10 minutes or until pasta is tender. Season to taste with black pepper.

2 Place egg yolks in a small bowl and whisk to combine. Whisk a little hot soup into egg yolks, then stir egg yolk mixture into soup. Serve immediately.

Serves 6

Vermicelli Onion Soup

$^{1}/_{4}$ cup/$^{1}/_{2}$ stick/60 g butter
3 onions, thinly sliced
1 tablespoon all-purpose flour
$1^{1}/_{4}$ cups/315 mL hot chicken stock
4 cups/1 liter milk
2 oz/60 g vermicelli, broken into pieces
freshly ground black pepper

1 Melt butter in a large saucepan and cook onions, stirring, over a medium heat for 6-7 minutes or until soft. Stir in flour, then gradually stir in hot stock. Cook, stirring constantly, for 4-5 minutes or until soup is smooth and thickened.

2 Stir in milk and bring to the boil. Add vermicelli and season to taste with black pepper. Cook, stirring frequently, for 8-10 minutes or until vermicelli is tender.

Serves 6

Vermicelli Onion Soup

CHILI CHICKEN SOUP

$3^1/_2$ oz/100 g fresh egg noodles
2 tablespoons peanut oil
2 onions, chopped
2 cloves garlic, crushed
1 red chili, finely sliced
1 teaspoon curry paste (vindaloo)
$^1/_4$ teaspoon ground turmeric
1 tablespoon finely chopped fresh lemon grass or 1 tablespoon finely grated lemon peel
4 cups/1 liter coconut milk
$1^1/_2$ cups/375 mL chicken stock
12 oz/375 g cooked chicken, chopped
3 large spinach leaves, finely shredded

1 Cook noodles in a large saucepan of boiling water for 3-4 minutes or until tender. Drain, then rinse noodles under cold running water. Drain again and place in individual serving bowls.

2 Heat oil in a large saucepan and cook onions for 2-3 minutes or until golden. Stir in garlic, chili, curry paste, turmeric and lemon grass, and cook for 1 minute.

3 Combine coconut milk and chicken stock. Add coconut milk mixture, chicken and spinach to pan. Bring to simmering and simmer for 3-4 minutes. Spoon soup over noodles in bowls and serve immediately.

Serves 6

Coconut milk can be purchased canned, or as a long-life product in cartons, or as a powder to which you add water. These products have a short life once opened and should be used within a day or so.

Chili Chicken Soup

You can make coconut milk using grated dry coconut and water. To make, place 1 lb/500 g grated dry coconut in a bowl and pour over 3 cups/750 mL of boiling water. Leave to stand for 30 minutes, then strain, squeezing the coconut to extract as much liquid as possible. This will make a thick coconut milk. The coconut can be used again to make a weaker coconut milk.

Italian Bean Soup

Italian Bean Soup

1 tablespoon olive oil
2 onions, chopped
2 cloves garlic, crushed
1 red pepper, chopped
6 cups/1.5 liters chicken or vegetable stock
$^3/_4$ cup/125 g small pasta shapes
$^1/_2$ cup/125 mL red wine
14 oz/440 g canned tomatoes, undrained and mashed
2 tablespoons tomato paste
10 oz/315 g canned red kidney beans, drained
freshly ground black pepper

1 Heat oil in a large saucepan and cook onions, garlic and red pepper for 4-5 minutes or until onion softens.

2 Stir in stock, pasta, wine, tomatoes, tomato paste and beans. Bring to the boil, then reduce heat and simmer for 15 minutes. Season to taste with black pepper.

Serves 6

Thick soups made with pulses and pasta are true peasant food. But they are just as good for filling hungry teenagers.

Chicken Noodle Soup

A homemade, well-seasoned, clear chicken broth filled with chicken, vegetables and noodles is a far cry from most of the packaged soups you buy in food shops.

4 cups/1 liter chicken stock
1 carrot, cut into matchsticks
1 leek, thinly sliced
4 oz/125 g cooked chicken, chopped
3 oz/90 g round egg noodles, broken into pieces
freshly ground black pepper
4 sprigs fresh coriander

1 Place stock in a large saucepan and bring to the boil. Add carrot and leek, cover, bring to simmering and simmer for 5 minutes or until carrot is tender.

2 Stir in chicken and noodles and cook for 5-10 minutes or until noodles are tender. Season to taste with black pepper. Serve garnished with coriander sprigs.

Serves 4

Chicken Noodle Soup

Chicken and Avocado Soup

Chicken and Avocado Soup

1 tablespoon/15 g butter
1 onion, finely chopped
1 large potato, diced
3 cups/750 mL chicken stock
10 oz/315 g canned sweet corn kernels, drained
12 oz/375 g cooked chicken, chopped
freshly ground black pepper
$^{1}/_{4}$ cup/60 mL light cream (half and half) or evaporated skim milk
1 avocado, peeled, pitted and diced

1 Melt butter in a large saucepan and cook onion for 2-3 minutes or until soft. Stir in potato and stock, cover, bring to simmering and simmer for 10-15 minutes or until potato is tender.

2 Add corn, chicken and black pepper to taste and cook for 5-6 minutes or until soup is hot. Spoon soup into individual serving bowls. Swirl in cream or milk and top with avocado. Serve immediately.

Serves 4

Chicken and avocados seem to go together like bread and butter, and no more so than in this substantial soup. For a wonderful luncheon, serve the soup with crusty bread and follow with a mixed green salad.

Thyme and Leek Soup

2 tablespoons/30 g butter
2 large leeks, white part only, chopped
2 potatoes, chopped
2 teaspoons chopped fresh thyme or 1/2 teaspoon dried thyme
4 cups/1 liter chicken stock
4 tablespoons whipping cream
sprigs fresh thyme

1 Melt butter in a large saucepan and cook leeks over a medium heat for 2-3 minutes. Add potatoes, thyme and stock. Bring to the boil, then reduce heat and simmer for 25 minutes or until potatoes are tender. Remove pan from heat and set aside to cool slightly.

2 Transfer soup mixture to a food processor or blender and process until smooth. Return soup to a clean saucepan and cook over a medium heat until hot. Ladle soup into warm bowls, place a tablespoon of cream in the center of each bowl and swirl using a skewer. Garnish with thyme sprigs and serve immediately.

Serves 4

Thyme is a highly fragrant herb of which there are many varieties. Common thyme is the one most used in cooking, but there are also lemon- , apple- and orange-scented thymes, to name but a few.

Thyme and Leek Soup

Dill and Carrot Soup

Dill and Carrot Soup

2 tablespoons/30 g butter
1 large onion, chopped
1 large sweet potato or potato, chopped
3 large carrots, chopped
4 cups/1 liter chicken or vegetable stock
$^3/_4$ cup/185 g dairy sour cream
2 tablespoons chopped fresh dill weed
sprigs fresh dill weed

1 Melt butter in a large saucepan and cook onion, sweet potato or potato and carrots for 5 minutes.

2 Stir in stock and bring to the boil, then reduce heat and simmer for 30 minutes. Remove pan from heat and set aside to cool slightly.

3 Transfer soup mixture, in batches, to a food processor or blender and process until smooth. To the last batch of soup mixture add the sour cream. Return soup to a clean saucepan and cook over a low heat, stirring constantly, until soup is hot. Do not allow the soup to boil or it will curdle. Stir in chopped dill weed and ladle soup into warmed bowls. Garnish with dill sprigs and serve immediately.

Serves 4

Dill weed and carrots have a natural affinity and no more so than in this delicious soup. This soup freezes well, but do not add the sour cream before freezing; stir it into the thawed soup just prior to reheating.

Creamy Tomato and Thyme Soup

2 tablespoons/30 g butter
2 onions, sliced
2 tablespoons finely chopped fresh thyme or 2 teaspoons dried thyme
1 leek, sliced
2 stalks celery, sliced
28 oz/810 g canned tomatoes, undrained and mashed
2 cups/500 mL chicken stock
$^1/_4$ cup/60 mL whipping cream
freshly ground black pepper
sprigs fresh thyme

Due to the acid content of tomatoes, creamy tomato soups have a tendency to curdle. To prevent this, mix a little of the hot soup with the cream before adding it to the soup.

1 Melt butter in a large saucepan and cook onions, thyme, leek and celery over a medium heat for 3-4 minutes or until vegetables are soft.

2 Stir in tomatoes and stock. Bring to the boil, then reduce heat and simmer for 30 minutes. Remove soup from heat and set aside to cool for 15 minutes. Place soup in a food processor or blender and process until smooth.

3 Return soup to a clean saucepan and heat over a medium heat for 4-5 minutes or until hot. Mix a little hot soup into cream, then mix cream mixture into soup. Season to taste with black pepper. Ladle soup into warm bowls, garnish with thyme sprigs and serve immediately.

Serves 4

Chilled Dill Soup

2 cups/500 mL chicken or vegetable stock
1 large onion, chopped
4 zucchini, chopped
1 large potato, chopped
$^1/_2$ teaspoon ground cumin
1 cup/250 g dairy sour cream
2 tablespoons chopped fresh dill weed
sprigs fresh dill weed

This soup is also delicious served hot. To serve hot, place processed soup mixture, sour cream and dill weed in a saucepan and cook over a medium heat, stirring constantly, until soup is hot. Do not allow the soup to boil or it will curdle.

1 Place stock, onion, zucchini, potato and cumin in a large saucepan and bring to the boil. Reduce heat and simmer for 20 minutes or until potatoes are tender. Remove saucepan from heat and set aside to cool slightly.

2 Place soup mixture in a food processor or blender and process until smooth. Transfer soup to a large bowl, stir in sour cream and chopped dill weed, then cover and chill for 3 hours before serving. Ladle soup into chilled bowls and garnish with dill sprigs.

Serves 4

Creamy Tomato and Thyme Soup

CHILLED TOMATO SOUP

6 large ripe tomatoes, peeled
2 cups/500 mL tomato juice
1 clove garlic, crushed
1 cucumber, peeled and chopped
4 spring onions, chopped
1 green pepper, chopped
2 stalks celery, chopped
1 tablespoon finely chopped fresh basil
freshly ground black pepper

1 Place tomatoes, tomato juice and garlic in a food processor or blender and process until smooth.

2 Transfer tomato mixture to a large bowl and stir in cucumber, spring onions, green pepper, celery, basil and black pepper to taste. Cover and refrigerate for 2-3 hours, or overnight, before serving.

Serves 6

This wonderful, uncooked soup is full of the tastes of summer. If possible, make it the day before to allow the flavors to develop. If good-flavored fresh tomatoes are unavailable, you can make this soup using a can of undrained, peeled tomatoes.

Right: Tom Yam Gong
Below: Creamy Mussel Soup

Creamy Mussel Soup

$2^1/2$ cups/600 mL dry white wine
1 teaspoon chili paste (sambal oelek)
2 tablespoons lemon juice
2 cloves garlic, crushed
1 lb/500 g fresh mussels, scrubbed and beards removed
$1^1/2$ cups/375 mL whipping cream
1 tablespoon chopped fresh dill weed
freshly ground black pepper

1 Place wine, chili paste (sambal oelek), lemon juice and garlic in a large saucepan and bring to the boil. Add mussels and cook for 5 minutes or until shells open. Discard any unopened mussels. Using a slotted spoon remove mussels from liquid and set aside.

2 Strain liquid through a fine sieve and return to a clean pan. Stir cream into wine mixture and bring to the boil. Reduce heat and simmer for 10 minutes.

3 Remove mussel meat from shells and stir into soup mixture. Add dill weed and season to taste with black pepper. Serve immediately.

Serves 4

Remember, any mussels that do not open their shells after 5 minutes of cooking should be discarded; they are bad.

Tom Yam Gong

3 cups/750 mL fish stock
1 tablespoon chopped fresh lemon grass or 1 teaspoon dried lemon grass
1/2 teaspoon finely grated lemon peel
2 tablespoons Thai fish sauce
8 oz/250 g button mushrooms, sliced
1 lb/500 g large uncooked shrimp, shelled and deveined
1/3 cup/90 mL whipping cream
4 oz/125 g bean sprouts
2 spring onions, cut into 3/4 in/2 cm lengths
1 teaspoon chili paste (sambal oelek)
1/3 cup/90 mL lemon juice
3 tablespoons chopped fresh coriander
freshly ground black pepper

1 Place stock in a large saucepan and bring to the boil. Stir in lemon grass, lemon peel, fish sauce, mushrooms and shrimp and cook for 3-4 minutes or until shrimp change color.

2 Reduce heat to low, stir in cream and cook for 2-3 minutes or until heated through.

3 Remove pan from heat, add bean sprouts, spring onions, chili paste (sambal oelek), lemon juice, coriander and black pepper to taste. Serve immediately.

Serves 4

When making the stock for this soup, include the shells of the shrimp to give a more intense flavor. Chicken stock can be used in place of the fish stock if you wish.

RECIPE COLLECTION

APPETIZERS

Choose a starter from this wonderful array of recipes for your next dinner party. Many of the dishes in this chapter also make great light meals when served with a salad and fresh bread or rolls.

Garlic and Rosemary Shrimp

Garlic and Rosemary Shrimp

2 lb/1 kg large uncooked shrimp, shelled and deveined
2 cloves garlic, crushed
1 tablespoon olive oil
freshly ground black pepper
2 sprigs fresh rosemary
2 tablespoons/30 g butter
1/2 cup/125 mL dry vermouth

1 Place shrimp, garlic, oil, black pepper to taste and rosemary in a large bowl and toss to combine. Cover and marinate in the refrigerator for 8 hours or overnight.

2 Melt butter in a large skillet and cook shrimp and marinade over a high heat for 2-3 minutes or until shrimp change color.

3 Using a slotted spoon, remove shrimp from pan and set aside. Discard rosemary sprigs. Stir vermouth into pan, bring to the boil and boil until mixture reduces and forms a glaze. Return shrimp to pan and toss to coat with glaze. Serve immediately.

Serves 4

While rosemary is most often associated with lamb, it is equally delicious with many other foods – including shrimp – as you will discover when you cook this dish.

Salmon and Chive Pate

2 teaspoons unflavored gelatin
2 tablespoons water
1/4 cup/60 mL tarragon vinegar
3 egg yolks
1/2 cup/1 stick/125 g butter
14 oz/440 g canned red salmon, drained, bones and skin removed and flaked
4 tablespoons snipped fresh chives
freshly ground black pepper

1 Sprinkle gelatin over water in a small bowl, place it over a small saucepan of simmering water and stir until gelatin dissolves. Set aside to cool at room temperature.

2 Place vinegar in a small saucepan, bring to the boil and boil until reduced to 2 tablespoons. Set aside to cool. Place vinegar and egg yolks in a food processor or blender and process to combine. Melt butter until hot and bubbling, taking care not to let it burn. With food processor running, slowly pour in melted butter and process until thick.

3 Place salmon, gelatin and butter mixtures in a bowl and mix to combine. Stir in chives and season to taste with black pepper.

Serves 8

An easy pâté that is perfect for last-minute entertaining and is just as good made with pink salmon or tuna. The chives give it a wonderfully subtle onion flavor. The flowers of the chive plant are also edible and their mauve color makes them a pretty garnish for soups, pâtés, dips and salads.

Smoked Salmon Salad

Smoked Salmon Salad

4 slices smoked salmon, cut into strips
2 avocados, pitted, peeled and thinly sliced
4 oz/125 g button mushrooms, thinly sliced

DILL DRESSING

1/4 cup/60 mL olive oil
1/2 teaspoon packed brown sugar
2 tablespoons freshly squeezed lemon juice
1 tablespoon dry white wine
1 tablespoon chopped fresh dill weed

1 To make dressing, place oil, sugar, lemon juice, wine and dill weed in a screwtop jar and shake well to combine.

2 Place salmon, avocados and mushrooms in a bowl, pour dressing over and toss gently. Serve immediately.

Serves 4

Dill weed was brought to America by the early settlers who called it 'meetin' seed' because the dill seed was given to children to chew on during long Sunday sermons.

Tomato Pesto Slices

4 large tomatoes, cut into 12 thick slices
12 slices mozzarella cheese, cut into rounds
6 slices cucumber, halved
6 black olives, pitted and halved
12 small sprigs fresh flat-leaved parsley

PESTO MAYONNAISE
1 large bunch fresh basil
1 clove garlic, crushed
2 oz/60 g pine nuts (pignola)
2 tablespoons olive oil
2 tablespoons grated fresh Parmesan cheese
2 tablespoons mayonnaise

1 To make mayonnaise, place basil leaves, garlic, pine nuts (pignola), oil and Parmesan cheese in a food processor or blender and process until smooth. Transfer mixture to a small bowl and stir in mayonnaise.

2 Top each tomato slice with a teaspoon of mayonnaise, then a slice of cheese, 1/2 a slice of cucumber, 1/2 an olive and a sprig of parsley.

Makes 12

Serve these strongly flavored, pesto-topped tomato slices with crusty Italian bread, followed by pasta topped with a garlic tomato sauce and a tossed green salad.

Tomato Pesto Slices

Coriander Mussel Tarts

Oven temperature
425°F, 220°C

The ancient Chinese believed that anyone who ate coriander would enjoy immortality; in the Middle East and Europe, coriander has long been valued as a love potion and aphrodisiac.

PASTRY

1 1/2 cups/185 g all-purpose flour
1/4 teaspoon baking powder
1/2 cup/1 stick/125 g butter, cubed and chilled
1 egg yolk
2-3 tablespoons iced water
1/2 teaspoon lemon juice

MUSSEL FILLING

16 mussels, in shells, scrubbed and debearded
1 leek, cut into thin strips
2 large carrots, cut into thin strips
1 tablespoon finely chopped fresh coriander
1 1/4 cups/315 mL whipping cream
12 uncooked shrimp, shelled and deveined
2 tablespoons flour
2 tablespoons/30 g softened butter
freshly ground black pepper

1 To make pastry, place flour, baking powder and butter in a food processor and process until mixture resembles coarse bread crumbs. Combine egg yolk, water and lemon juice. With machine running, gradually pour in egg mixture, until a soft dough forms. Turn dough onto a lightly floured surface and knead gently. Wrap dough in plastic wrap and refrigerate for 1 hour.

2 Divide pastry into four portions and roll out thinly on a lightly floured surface. Line four 4 in/10 cm tart pans with pastry and prick base of each tart with a fork. Line tarts with parchment paper and fill with uncooked rice. Bake for 5 minutes, remove paper and rice, and bake for 12 minutes longer.

3 To make filling, place mussels in a large saucepan, add just enough water to cover and cook over a low heat until shells open. Discard any mussels that have not opened. Using a slotted spoon remove mussels from liquid. Remove mussel meat from shells and discard shells. Reserve 1/2 cup/125 mL of pan liquid. Heat reserved liquid in a skillet, add leek, carrots and coriander, and cook for 2 minutes.

4 Stir in cream, shrimp and mussels, and cook over a low heat for 5 minutes. Mix flour and butter together to form a paste, then whisk small quantities of paste gradually into cream mixture and cook, stirring, for 2-3 minutes or until thickened and smooth. Season to taste with black pepper. Spoon filling into warm pastry shells and serve immediately.

Serves 4

Coriander Mussel Tarts

Gravlax

Gravlax

$1^{1}/_{2}$ lb/750 g salmon fillet, bones and skin removed
2 cups/500 mL rosé wine
2 teaspoons finely grated orange peel
2 teaspoons finely grated lime peel
2 tablespoons chopped fresh coriander
1 tablespoon cracked black pepper
2 tablespoons chopped fresh dill weed
4 tablespoons coarse sea salt
$^{1}/_{2}$ cup/90 g packed brown sugar
$^{1}/_{2}$ cup/125 mL olive oil

1 Place salmon in a shallow dish. Place wine, orange peel and lime peel in a small bowl, mix to combine and pour over salmon. Cover and refrigerate for 24 hours.

2 Remove salmon from wine mixture and pat dry using paper towels. Place coriander, black pepper, dill weed, salt and sugar in a small bowl and mix to combine. Brush salmon with half the oil and sprinkle with half the coriander mixture. Place salmon herbed side down on a large piece of aluminum foil. Brush other side with remaining oil and sprinkle with remaining coriander mixture. Wrap salmon tightly in foil and refrigerate for 2 days. Serve cut into thin slices.

Serves 6

While this dish needs to be prepared several days ahead, you will be well pleased with the result. Gravlax makes a delicious first course served with thin slices of lemon and rye bread.

Trout Seviche

This recipe is also delicious made with other fish. Choose any firm white fish fillets in place of the trout, or for something really special you might like to make the salad using fresh salmon.
To avoid the risk of food poisoning do not use shellfish such as shrimp or mussels for this recipe.

1 lb/500 g trout fillets, skin and bones removed, flesh cut into bite-sized pieces
1 teaspoon finely grated lemon peel
1/4 cup/60 mL lemon juice
1 teaspoon finely grated lime peel
1/4 cup/60 mL lime juice
1/2 cup/125 mL dry vermouth
2 tablespoons finely chopped fresh dill weed
freshly ground black pepper
6 lettuce cups or lettuce leaves

1 Place trout, lemon peel, lemon juice, lime peel, lime juice, vermouth, dill weed and black pepper to taste in a bowl and toss to combine. Cover and refrigerate for at least 8 hours or overnight. Stir occasionally during marinating.

2 To serve, divide fish mixture between lettuce cups or line a salad bowl with lettuce leaves and top with fish mixture.

Serves 6

Calamari with Curry Sauce

1 lb/500 g calamari (squid) rings
1/2 cup/60 g cornstarch
vegetable oil for deep-frying

CURRY SAUCE
1 tablespoon vegetable oil
1 small onion, finely chopped
2 cloves garlic, crushed
1 tablespoon curry powder
2 tablespoons plum sauce or sweet and sour sauce
2 teaspoons soy sauce
1/2 cup/125 mL water
1 tablespoon lemon juice
2 teaspoons packed brown sugar
2 tablespoons chopped fresh coriander
freshly ground black pepper

1 To make sauce, heat oil in a small saucepan and cook onion and garlic for 4-5 minutes or until onion is soft. Add curry powder and cook, stirring, for 1 minute longer. Stir in plum sauce, soy sauce, water, lemon juice and sugar, bring to simmering and cook, stirring occasionally, until sauce is reduced by half. Remove pan from heat and set aside to cool. Stir in coriander and season to taste with black pepper.

2 Toss calamari (squid) in cornstarch. Heat oil in a large saucepan over a high heat and cook calamari (squid) a few at a time for 2-3 minutes or until lightly browned. Using a slotted spoon remove calamari (squid) and drain on paper towels. Serve immediately with sauce for dipping.

Serves 6

Either fresh or frozen calamari (squid) rings can be used for this dish. Freezing calamari (squid) has no adverse effect on it – in fact more often than not it tenderizes it.

Trout Seviche,
Calamari with Curry Sauce

Curried Fish Parcels

20 long fresh chives, blanched

CURRY CREPES

1 cup/125 g all-purpose flour
2 eggs
1/2 cup/125 mL milk
1/2 cup/125 mL water
2 teaspoons curry powder
1 teaspoon ground cumin
2 tablespoons/30 g butter, melted

COCONUT FISH FILLING

1 tablespoon vegetable oil
1 clove garlic, crushed
1 small onion, finely chopped
1 teaspoon finely grated fresh ginger
6 oz/185 g firm white fish fillets, cut into cubes
1 tablespoon grated dry coconut
1 tablespoon whipping cream
freshly ground black pepper

1 To make crêpes, place flour, eggs, milk, water, curry powder, cumin and butter in a food processor or blender and process for 1 minute. Set batter aside to stand for 1 hour.

2 Pour 1 tablespoon batter into a heated, lightly greased 7-7 1/2 in/18-19 cm crêpe pan or skillet and cook over a medium heat for 30 seconds each side or until lightly browned. Remove crêpe from pan and repeat with remaining batter to make 20 crêpes.

3 To make filling, heat oil in a large skillet and cook garlic, onion and ginger over a medium heat for 3-4 minutes or until onion is soft. Add fish, coconut and cream and cook, stirring, for 4-5 minutes or until fish is just cooked. Remove pan from heat and set aside to cool to room temperature. Place 2 teaspoons filling in the middle of each crêpe, gather up edges and tie with a chive to form a parcel or bag. Serve at room temperature.

Makes 20

The crêpes can be made in advance and frozen if you wish. To freeze, stack cold crêpes between sheets of waxed paper or freezer wrap and place in a sealed freezer bag, or wrap tightly in aluminum foil. Defrost crêpes at room temperature before using.

Smoked Salmon Rolls

20 thin slices smoked salmon
20 sprigs fresh dill weed

CREAM CHEESE FILLING

5 oz/155 g smoked salmon, chopped
1/3 cup/90 mL whipping cream
1 tablespoon lemon juice
1 tablespoon bottled horseradish
8 oz/250 g cream cheese
freshly ground black pepper

1 To make filling, place smoked salmon, cream, lemon juice, horseradish, cream cheese and black pepper to taste in a food processor or blender and process until smooth.

2 Place 2 teaspoons filling along one side of each smoked salmon slice, then roll up to form a tube. Place rolls seam side down on a large serving platter and top each roll with a dill sprig.

Makes 20

These rolls are also delicious made with smoked trout instead of the smoked salmon. They can be made 2-3 hours ahead of serving and stored, covered, in the refrigerator until you are ready to serve them.

Curried Fish Parcels,
Smoked Salmon Rolls

Anchovy Dip

1 1/4 cups/300 g dairy sour cream or plain yogurt
1 1/2 oz/45 g canned anchovy fillets, drained and mashed
3 tablespoons finely chopped dill pickles
freshly ground black pepper
2 teaspoons chopped capers

1 Place sour cream or yogurt, anchovy fillets, dill pickles and black pepper to taste in a food processor or blender and process to combine.

2 Transfer dip to a bowl and garnish with capers.

Serves 6-8

Served with crackers, raw vegetable sticks or Melba toast, this is one of the easiest and tastiest starters that you will ever make.

Oysters with Caviar

36 small oysters on the half-shell
4 tablespoons black caviar or lumpfish roe
fresh dill weed sprigs

HORSERADISH MAYONNAISE
2 tablespoons mayonnaise or dairy sour cream
1 teaspoon lemon juice
1 teaspoon tomato paste
2 teaspoons bottled horseradish
freshly ground black pepper

You may like to serve the mayonnaise separately and so allow each person to add their own if they wish.

1 Arrange oysters on a large serving platter and set the platter on a bed of ice.

2 To make Horseradish Mayonnaise, place mayonnaise or sour cream, lemon juice, tomato paste, horseradish and black pepper to taste in a small bowl and mix to combine.

3 Top each oyster with a little mayonnaise, a little caviar, or lumpfish roe, and garnish with a dill sprig.

Makes 36

Oysters Rockefeller

It is believed that this dish was created in the late 1800s at Antoine's, a well-known New Orleans restaurant. The name of the dish is said to have originated from a customer remarking that oysters prepared in this way were 'as rich as Rockefeller'.

36 small oysters on the half-shell
1 lb/500 g fresh spinach, chopped
1 cup/250 g dairy sour cream
2 cloves garlic, crushed
freshly ground black pepper
3 tablespoons finely shredded mature Cheddar cheese
1/2 cup/30 g fresh bread crumbs

1 Remove oysters from shells and reserve both flesh and shells.

2 Boil, steam or microwave spinach until cooked, then drain well and place in a sieve. Using the back of a spoon, press spinach to remove as much moisture as possible.

3 Place sour cream, garlic and spinach in a bowl and mix to combine. Season to taste with black pepper. Place a teaspoon of spinach mixture in each oyster shell, then top with a reserved oyster. Top with another teaspoon of spinach mixture.

4 Place cheese and bread crumbs in a small bowl and mix to combine. Sprinkle bread crumb mixture over oysters and cook under a preheated broiler for 3-4 minutes or until cheese melts and topping is browned.

Makes 36

Oysters with Caviar

Creamy Oyster Dip

Creamy Oyster Dip

1/2 cup/125 mL thick cream
1/4 cup/60 mL milk
1/2 cup/125 g dairy sour cream
2 tablespoons tomato catsup
1 teaspoon cornstarch
freshly ground black pepper
24 small oysters, removed from shells, or 24 bottled oysters, drained

1 Place cream, milk, sour cream, catsup, cornstarch and black pepper to taste in a small saucepan and whisk to combine. Cook cream mixture over a low heat, stirring constantly, for 4-5 minutes or until mixture thickens.

2 Remove sauce from heat and stir in oysters. Serve immediately.

Serves 4

This dip is delicious served with Melba toast, crackers or thin slices of rye bread. To make Melba toast, cut bread into slices of a medium thickness and lightly toast. Cut crusts from toast and split each slice of toast horizontally. Cut each slice in half diagonally and bake at 350°F/180°C for 5-7 minutes or until the edges curl and the toast is golden.

Spiked Cheese Balls

2 tablespoons vodka
3 slices stale rye or brown bread, crumbed
4 oz/125 g blue cheese
4 oz/125 g cream cheese
1/4 cup/1/2 stick/60 g butter, softened
1 tablespoon caraway seeds
1/4 cup/30 g almonds, toasted and coarsely ground

These delicious morsels are easy to make and will keep in an airtight container in the refrigerator for up to one week. They are a great gift for cheese-lovers.

1 Place vodka and 2 tablespoons bread crumbs in a bowl and set aside to stand for 5 minutes.

2 Place blue cheese, cream cheese and butter in a food processor or blender and process to combine. Transfer cheese mixture to a bowl, add bread crumb mixture and mix to combine. Cover and chill for 30 minutes or until mixture is firm enough to handle.

3 Place caraway seeds and remaining bread crumbs in a bowl. Place almonds in a separate bowl. Take about 2 teaspoons cheese mixture and roll into a ball. Repeat with remaining mixture to make about 60 balls. Roll half the cheese balls in the bread crumb mixture and half in the almonds. Place cheese balls on a plate lined with plastic wrap and chill until firm.

Makes **60**

Olive Cheese Balls

1 cup/125 g shredded mature Cheddar cheese, at room temperature
3 tablespoons/45 g butter, softened
1/2 cup/60 g all-purpose flour
1/2 teaspoon cayenne pepper
25-30 pitted or stuffed olives

1 Place cheese and butter in a bowl and beat until creamy. Sift in flour and cayenne pepper and knead to make a firm dough.

2 Wrap a teaspoon of dough around each olive and place on a lightly greased baking sheet. Bake for 15 minutes or until golden. Remove balls from sheet and cool on a wire rack.

Makes 25-30

Oven temperature
400°F, 200°C

These unusual cheese balls are great to serve with drinks or as an interesting addition to a cheeseboard. They will keep in an airtight container for up to one week.

Cheese and Walnut Pate

1/2 cup/1 stick/125 g butter, at room temperature
3 cups/375 g shredded mature Cheddar cheese
1/2 cup/125 mL beer
1/2 teaspoon Dijon mustard
1 teaspoon Worcestershire sauce
freshly ground black pepper
1 cup/90 g walnut halves

1 Place butter in a bowl and beat until light and fluffy. Mix cheese and beer, alternately, into butter and beat until well combined.

2 Stir in mustard, Worcestershire sauce and black pepper to taste.

3 Line a small dish with plastic wrap, so that the wrap comes up the sides of the container and hangs over the sides. Place half the walnuts in base of container. Cover with half the cheese mixture, then top with remaining walnuts and cheese mixture. Smooth top of cheese, cover and refrigerate for 24 hours. To serve, turn out onto a serving plate and remove plastic wrap.

Makes 1 lb/500 g

This pâté will keep, covered, in the refrigerator for up to 10 days and so is great for entertaining as you can make it days in advance. Rather than make one big pâté you might like to make individual ones for an elegant appetizer. Simply divide the mixture between individual soufflé or custard cups and serve with a selection of crackers and fresh or dried fruit.

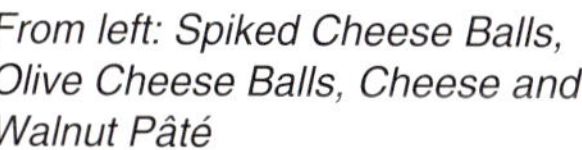
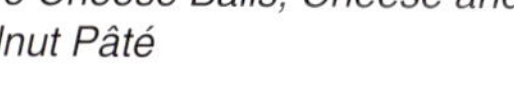

From left: Spiked Cheese Balls, Olive Cheese Balls, Cheese and Walnut Pâté

Cheese Cigars

A pesto made with coriander is perfect with these tasty Cheese Cigars – serve them as an indulgent pre-dinner treat or snack. They are ideal for entertaining as they need to be refrigerated before cooking.

12 slices white sandwich bread, crusts removed
2 teaspoons prepared hot English mustard
4 tablespoons finely grated fresh Parmesan cheese
$^1/_2$ cup/60 g shredded mozzarella cheese
1 tablespoon snipped fresh chives
cayenne pepper
1 egg, lightly beaten
vegetable oil for deep-frying

CORIANDER PESTO

3 large bunches/9$^1/_2$ oz/300 g fresh coriander
2 cloves garlic, crushed
2 oz/60 g pine nuts (pignola)
$^1/_2$ cup/125 mL olive oil
$^1/_2$ cup/60 g grated fresh Parmesan cheese
freshly ground black pepper

1 Roll each slice of bread with a rolling pin to flatten as much as possible.

2 Place mustard, Parmesan cheese, mozzarella cheese, chives and cayenne pepper to taste in a bowl and mix well to combine. Divide cheese mixture between bread slices and spread over half of each bread slice. Brush unspread half of bread slices with egg. Roll each slice up tightly using the egg to seal rolls. Arrange rolls side by side on a tray lined with plastic wrap, cover and refrigerate for 15 minutes or until ready to cook.

3 To make pesto, place coriander leaves, garlic and pine nuts (pignola) in a food processor or blender and process until finely chopped. With machine running, slowly pour in oil and process mixture until smooth. Add Parmesan cheese and black pepper to taste and process to combine.

4 Heat 1 in/2.5 cm oil in a large skillet. When hot, cook cigars a few at a time until evenly golden all over. Drain on paper towels. Serve cigars immediately with pesto.

Makes 12

Cheese Cigars

Pear and Prosciutto Salad

3 pears, peeled, cored and quartered
2 tablespoons lemon juice
12 slices prosciutto or lean ham
$3^1/2$ oz/100 g mozzarella cheese
freshly ground black pepper
2 tablespoons olive oil
sprigs flat-leaved parsley

1 Brush each pear quarter with lemon juice and wrap in a slice of prosciutto or ham. Using a vegetable peeler, peel off slivers of mozzarella cheese.

2 Arrange three prosciutto- or ham-wrapped pear quarters and some cheese slivers on each serving plate. Season to taste with black pepper, drizzle with oil and garnish with parsley sprigs. Serve immediately.

Serves 4

This salad is also delicious made with apples in place of the pears.

Avocado and Stilton Salad

1 large avocado, quartered and pitted
2 tablespoons lemon juice
4 slices lemon, halved
½ bunch/4 oz/125 g watercress
pinch paprika

STILTON DRESSING
2½ oz/75 g Stilton or blue cheese
¼ cup/60 mL olive oil
2 tablespoons lemon juice
1 small clove garlic, crushed
freshly ground black pepper
½ cup/125 mL whipping cream

1 Cut each avocado quarter into three or four slices lengthwise, taking care not to cut right through at the narrow end. Fan out avocado quarters and arrange on four serving plates. Brush avocados with lemon juice. Garnish plates with lemon slices and watercress sprigs.

2 To make dressing, place cheese, oil, lemon juice, garlic and black pepper to taste in a food processor or blender and process until smooth. Transfer cheese mixture to a bowl and stir in cream. Spoon dressing over avocado and sprinkle with a little paprika. Serve immediately.

Serves 4

The dressing for this elegant starter can be prepared in advance leaving only the cutting of the avocado to be done just prior to serving.

Avocado and Stilton Salad

Smoked Trout and Chili Salad

1 smoked trout, skin and head removed
2 ripe mangoes or nectarines, flesh cut into thin strips
1 oz/30 g coriander or flat-leaved parsley sprigs

CHILI DRESSING
$^{1}/_{2}$-1 tablespoon chili sauce
1 teaspoon packed brown sugar
4-5 tablespoons olive oil
2 tablespoons lemon juice
freshly ground black pepper

1 Remove bones from trout and break flesh into pieces.

2 Arrange trout, mango or nectarine strips and coriander or parsley on a large serving platter or on individual plates.

3 To make dressing, place chili sauce, sugar, oil, lemon juice and black pepper to taste in a screwtop jar and shake well to combine. Spoon dressing over salad and serve immediately.

Serves 4

This salad can be prepared in advance; simply arrange trout, mango and coriander or parsley sprigs on plates, cover with plastic wrap and refrigerate. Make up dressing and store in refrigerator. Just prior to serving, spoon dressing over salad.

Smoked Trout and Chili Salad

Fettuccine with Coriander Sauce

1 lb/500 g fettuccine

CORIANDER SAUCE
2 cloves garlic, chopped
2/3 cup/60 g walnut pieces
2 oz/60 g fresh coriander leaves
1/2 oz/15 g fresh parsley leaves
4-5 tablespoons vegetable oil
1/2 cup/60 g grated Parmesan cheese
freshly ground black pepper

1 Cook fettuccine in boiling water in a large saucepan following package directions. Drain, set aside and keep warm.

2 To make sauce, place garlic, walnuts, coriander and parsley in a food processor or blender and process to finely chop. With machine running, add oil in a steady stream. Add Parmesan cheese and black pepper to taste, and process to combine.

3 Spoon sauce over pasta and toss to combine. Serve immediately.

Serves 6

Coriander, a member of the carrot family, is indigenous to the Mediterranean. Also known as cilantro and Chinese parsley, it has a fresh taste and is popular in Indian, Asian, Mexican, South American and Middle Eastern cooking.

Garlic Spaghetti with Watercress

9 1/2 oz/300 g spaghetti
1/4 cup/1/2 stick/60 g butter
3 cloves garlic, crushed
2 oz/60 g watercress sprigs
4 tablespoons grated Parmesan cheese
freshly ground black pepper

1 Cook spaghetti in boiling water in a large saucepan following package directions. Drain, set aside and keep warm.

2 Melt butter in a large skillet and cook garlic, over a low heat, for 3-4 minutes. Remove pan from heat and add spaghetti, watercress and Parmesan cheese. Season to taste with black pepper and toss to combine. Serve immediately.

Serves 4

When cooking garlic it is important to use a low heat so that the garlic does not brown or burn. Burned garlic has an unpleasant, bitter taste.

Fettuccine with Coriander Sauce

Tomato Pasta Rolls

When the menu calls for finger food, and something a little more substantial is required, these rolls are ideal. Or serve individual slices with a small green salad as a colorful first course for a dinner party. Either way, the time taken to make these will be well rewarded.

2 cups/250 g all-purpose flour
2 eggs
2 tablespoons water
3 tablespoons tomato paste
1 tablespoon olive oil

SPINACH FILLING
1 lb/500 g frozen spinach, thawed and well drained
12 oz/375 g ricotta or dry cottage cheese
2 eggs
3/4 cup/90 g grated Parmesan cheese
1 teaspoon ground nutmeg
freshly ground black pepper
12 slices prosciutto or thinly sliced ham
1 lb/500 g sliced mozzarella cheese

1 Place flour, eggs, water, tomato paste and oil in a food processor and process to combine. Turn dough onto a lightly floured surface and knead for 5 minutes or until dough is smooth and elastic. Wrap dough in plastic wrap and set aside to stand for 15 minutes.

2 To make filling, place spinach, ricotta cheese, eggs, Parmesan cheese, nutmeg and black pepper to taste in a bowl, and mix to combine.

3 Divide dough in half and roll out one half to form a rectangle 12 x 18 in/30 x 45 cm. Spread with half the filling mixture, leaving a 1 in/2.5 cm border, then top with half the prosciutto or ham and half the mozzarella cheese. Fold in borders on long sides, then roll up from the short side. Wrap roll in a piece of washed calico cloth and secure ends with string. Repeat with remaining ingredients to make a second roll.

4 Half fill a flameproof baking dish with water and place on the stove top. Bring to the boil, add rolls, reduce heat, cover dish with aluminum foil or lid and simmer for 30 minutes. Turn rolls once or twice during cooking. Remove rolls from water and allow to cool for 5 minutes. Remove calico from rolls and refrigerate until firm. To serve, cut rolls into slices.

Serves 12

Tomato Pasta Rolls

Spaghetti and Pesto

1 lb/500 g spaghetti

PESTO

4 oz/125 g fresh basil leaves
4 tablespoons pine nuts (pignola)
4 cloves garlic, crushed
$^{1}/_{3}$ cup/90 mL olive oil
freshly ground black pepper

1 Cook spaghetti in boiling water in a large saucepan following package directions. Drain, set aside and keep warm.

2 To make Pesto, place basil, pine nuts (pignola) and garlic in a food processor or blender and process to finely chop all ingredients. With machine running, add oil in a steady steam. Season to taste with black pepper.

3 Add Pesto to spaghetti and toss to combine. Serve immediately.

Serves 6

Pesto is delicious served with any ribbon pasta. You might like to use fettuccine, tagliatelle or pappardelle in place of the spaghetti in this recipe. Pesto is also wonderful stirred into vegetable soups, tossed through steamed or microwaved vegetables and added to mayonnaise to make an interesting dressing for potato salad.

Spaghetti and Pesto

Smoked Salmon Fettuccine

1 lb/500 g fettuccine

SMOKED SALMON SAUCE
4 oz/125 g fresh or frozen peas
$^1/_4$ cup/60 mL white wine
$1^1/_4$ cups/315 mL whipping cream
8 slices smoked salmon
3 spring onions, finely chopped
freshly ground black pepper

1 Cook fettuccine in boiling water in a large saucepan following package directions. Drain, set aside and keep warm.

2 To make sauce, blanch peas in boiling water for 2 minutes. Refresh under cold running water, drain and set aside. Place wine in a large skillet and bring to the boil. Stir in 1 cup/250 mL cream and boil until sauce reduces and thickens. Place 4 slices smoked salmon, spring onions and remaining cream in a food processor and purée. Stir smoked salmon mixture into sauce and cook until sauce is hot.

3 Cut remaining salmon slices into strips. Add salmon strips and peas to sauce and season to taste with black pepper. Spoon sauce over fettuccine and toss to combine. Serve immediately.

Serves 6

Smoked Salmon Fettuccine

Chicken and Leek Rolls

12 spinach lasagne sheets
2 tablespoons grated fresh Parmesan cheese

CHICKEN AND LEEK FILLING
2 teaspoons vegetable oil
3 leeks, finely sliced
3 boned, skinned chicken breast halves, cut into thin strips
$^1/_2$ cup/125 mL chicken stock
1 tablespoon cornstarch blended with 2 tablespoons water
1 teaspoon French mustard
2 teaspoons chopped fresh basil
freshly ground black pepper

1 Cook lasagne sheets in boiling water in a large saucepan until tender. Drain, set aside and keep warm.

2 To make filling, heat oil in a large skillet and cook leeks and chicken, stirring, for 4-5 minutes or until chicken is brown. Stir in stock, cornstarch mixture, mustard and basil and cook, stirring, for 2 minutes longer. Season to taste with black pepper.

3 Place spoonfuls of filling on lasagne sheets, roll up, top with Parmesan cheese and serve immediately.

Serves 6

Chicken and Leek Rolls

Country Terrine

Oven temperature
350°F, 180°C

1 1/2 lb/750 g ground pork and veal
1 onion, finely chopped
2 cloves garlic, crushed
4 large spinach leaves, shredded
10 pitted prunes, roughly chopped
1 large green apple, finely diced
2 oz/60 g pine nuts (pignola)
1/4 cup/60 mL brandy
1/4 cup/30 g all-purpose flour
1/2 cup/125 mL whipping cream
2 teaspoons chopped fresh parsley
freshly ground black pepper
1 lb/500 g sliced bacon

1 Place pork and veal, onion, garlic, spinach, prunes, apple, pine nuts (pignola), brandy, flour, cream, parsley and black pepper to taste in a large bowl and mix to combine.

2 Line a lightly greased 4 1/2 x 8 1/2 in/11 x 21 cm loaf pan with bacon slices allowing slices to overhang the top. Pack meat mixture into loaf pan and smooth top. Fold overhanging bacon into the center to cover filling. Cover pan tightly with a double thickness of aluminum foil. Place in a baking dish with enough hot water to come halfway up sides of pan and cook for 1 1/2 hours or until mixture is coming away from sides of pan and is cooked through.

3 Remove foil, drain off excess liquid and refrigerate overnight.

Serves 10

This terrine is also excellent as a lunch or picnic dish when served with crusty French bread and mango chutney.

Fruity Pork Roulade

4 thick lean pork rib chops, boned and butterflied
2 cups/500 mL beef stock
4 stalks celery, chopped
2 onions, chopped

FRUIT FILLING
2 oz/60 g pine nuts (pignola)
1/2 cup/100 g pitted prunes
1/2 cup/60 g dried apricots
1 tablespoon grated fresh ginger
1 teaspoon chopped fresh sage
1/4 cup/60 g fruit chutney
4 slices bacon, chopped
1/4 cup/60 mL brandy
freshly ground black pepper

1 To make filling, place pine nuts (pignola), prunes, apricots, ginger, sage, chutney, bacon, brandy and black pepper to taste in a food processor and process until finely chopped.

2 Open out chops and pound to about 1/4 in/5 mm thick. Spread filling over steaks and roll up tightly. Secure each roll with string.

3 Place stock, celery and onions in a large saucepan and bring to the boil. Add pork rolls, cover and simmer for 20 minutes or until pork is cooked. Transfer pork rolls to a plate, set aside to cool, then cover and refrigerate for 2-3 hours. To serve, cut each roll into slices.

Serves 6

Perfect finger food to serve with pre-dinner drinks. Served on a bed of mixed lettuces, these pork slices also make an elegant starter.

Country Terrine

RECIPE COLLECTION

MAIN DISHES

In this chapter you will find dishes to suit all occasions. Whether it's a hearty family casserole, a roast for a special occasion or a simple pasta dish for quick entertaining, you are sure to find it here.

Beef in Red Wine

Beef in Red Wine

5 oz/155 g bacon, cut into strips
1 tablespoon vegetable oil
2 lb/1 kg chuck or blade steak, cut into 1 in/2.5 cm cubes
2 carrots, sliced
1 onion, sliced
1/4 cup/30 g all-purpose flour
freshly ground black pepper
1 1/2 cups/375 mL red wine
1 cup/250 mL beef stock
2 tablespoons tomato paste
2 cloves garlic, crushed
1 teaspoon dried thyme
1 bay leaf
2 tablespoons/30 g butter
18 small boiling onions
18 button mushrooms

Serves 6

1 Place bacon in a large flameproof casserole or Dutch oven and cook for 2 minutes. Remove bacon and drain on paper towels. Add oil to casserole and cook beef in batches for 4-5 minutes or until browned. Remove and set aside. Add carrots and sliced onion and cook for 4-5 minutes.

2 Drain excess fat from casserole and return bacon and meat to dish. Add flour and black pepper to taste, toss to combine and cook for 2 minutes longer. Stir in wine, stock, tomato paste, garlic, thyme and bay leaf, bring to the boil, then transfer to a preheated oven and cook for 1 1/2 hours.

3 Melt butter in a large skillet and cook small onions over a medium heat for 10 minutes. Remove, add to casserole and cook for 30 minutes longer. Add mushrooms to pan and cook for 3-4 minutes. Stir into casserole.

Oven temperature
300°F, 150°C

Lean meat plays an important part in a balanced diet. Lean beef, lamb and pork are highly nutritious. A 4 oz/125 g cooked serve provides much of the daily requirement of protein, the B-group vitamins, iron and zinc.

Osso Bucco

1 tablespoon olive oil
2 red peppers, cut into strips
2 onions, chopped
4 thick veal shank cross cuts
1/2 cup/60 g all-purpose flour
2 tablespoons/30 g butter
1/2 cup/125 mL dry white wine
1/2 cup/125 mL chicken stock
14 oz/440 g canned tomatoes, undrained and mashed
freshly ground black pepper
1 tablespoon chopped fresh parsley

Serves 4

1 Heat oil in a large skillet and cook red peppers and onions over a medium heat for 10 minutes or until onions are transparent. Using a slotted spoon, remove onion mixture and set aside. Toss veal in flour and shake off excess. Add butter to skillet and cook until butter foams. Add veal and cook for 4-5 minutes each side or until browned.

2 Stir in wine and stock and bring to the boil, stirring to lift sediment from base of pan. Boil until liquid is reduced by half. Add tomatoes and return onion mixture to pan, cover and simmer for 1 hour or until meat falls away from the bone. Season to taste with black pepper and sprinkle with parsley.

The name of this dish means 'hollow bones' and is a specialty from the Italian town of Milan.

Spicy Braised Beef

4 lb/2 kg boneless chuck eye roast, rump roast or round tip roast, in one piece
$^1/_2$ cup/60 g all-purpose flour
2 tablespoons/30 g ghee or clarified butter
3 onions, chopped
3 cloves garlic, crushed
1 tablespoon grated fresh ginger
1 teaspoon finely grated lemon peel
3 tablespoons curry powder
1 cup/250 mL tamarind liquid
1 lb/500 g plain yogurt
$^1/_2$ cup/45 g grated dry coconut
1 cup/250 mL coconut milk

RED DHAL

1 cup/200 g red lentils, washed
2 cups/500 mL water
1 stick cinnamon
3 whole cloves
1 teaspoon black peppercorns, cracked
2 tablespoons/30 g ghee or clarified butter
2 onions, sliced
1 teaspoon ground coriander
1 teaspoon ground cumin
1 teaspoon ground cardamom
1 teaspoon chili paste (sambal oelek)
3 cloves garlic, crushed
1 cup/90 g grated dry coconut

1 Toss beef in flour and shake off excess. Melt ghee or butter in a large saucepan and cook beef over a high heat until browned on all sides. Add onions, garlic, ginger, lemon peel, curry powder, tamarind liquid, yogurt and coconut to pan, cover and gently simmer for $1^1/_2$-2 hours or until meat is tender. Stir in coconut milk and simmer for 15 minutes longer.

2 To make dhal, place lentils, water, cinnamon, cloves and peppercorns in a large saucepan and bring to the boil, then reduce heat and simmer for 30 minutes or until lentils are cooked. Remove cinnamon and cloves and discard.

3 Melt ghee or butter in a skillet and cook onions, coriander, cumin, cardamom, chili paste (sambal oelek), garlic and coconut over medium heat for 4-5 minutes or until onion is golden. Stir onion mixture into lentil mixture.

4 Remove beef from cooking liquid and set aside to rest in a warm place for 15 minutes. Return pan to heat, bring liquid to the boil and boil rapidly for 5-10 minutes or until liquid thickens. Serve beef cut into slices with gravy and accompany with dhal.

Serves 8

Tamarind is the large pod of the tamarind or Indian date tree. After picking, it is seeded and peeled then pressed into a dark brown pulp.
To make tamarind liquid, mix tamarind with warm water then use in chutneys, sauces, curries or recipes such as this one. Tamarind is available from Asian food shops.
If tamarind is unavailable use 1 cup/250 mL beef stock in place of the tamarind liquid. The taste will be different but still delicious.

'Tamarind is the large pod of the Indian tamarind tree. It is usually mixed with warm water to make tamarind juice or liquid.'

Spicy Braised Beef

Above: Apple Pork Casserole
Right: Cassoulet

Apple Pork Casserole

2 tablespoons/30 g butter
2 onions, chopped
1 lb/500 g lean diced pork
3 large apples, peeled, cored and chopped
1 tablespoon dried mixed herbs
3 cups/750 mL chicken stock
freshly ground black pepper

APPLE SAUCE
2 tablespoons/30 g butter
2 apples, peeled, cored and chopped
2 tablespoons snipped fresh chives
14 oz/440 g canned tomatoes, undrained and mashed
1 teaspoon cracked black peppercorns

1 Heat butter in a large skillet and cook onions and pork over a medium heat for 5 minutes. Add apples, herbs, stock and black pepper to taste, bring to the boil, then reduce heat and simmer for 1 hour or until pork is tender. Using a slotted spoon, remove pork and set aside.

2 Push liquid and solids through a sieve and return to pan with pork.

3 To make sauce, melt butter in a skillet and cook apple over a medium heat for 2 minutes. Stir in chives and tomatoes and bring to the boil, reduce heat and simmer for 5 minutes. Pour into pan with pork and cook over a medium heat for 5 minutes longer. Just prior to serving, sprinkle with cracked black peppercorns.

Serves 4

This recipe is also delicious made using lean diced lamb in place of the pork. Serve with boiled brown or white rice and a green vegetable such as cabbage or beans.

Cassoulet

2 tablespoons olive oil
3 oz/90 g bacon, chopped
2 onions, chopped
4 cloves garlic, crushed
1 lb/500 g lean pork, cut into 2 in/5 cm pieces
1 lb/500 g lean lamb, cut into 2 in/5 cm pieces
1 lb/500 g thick pork sausages
1 lb/500 g canned lima beans
28 oz/810 g canned tomato purée
4 tomatoes, peeled and chopped
2 tablespoons chopped fresh sage or 2 teaspoons dried sage
2 tablespoons chopped fresh thyme or 2 teaspoons dried thyme
1 cup/250 mL beef stock
1 cup/250 mL red wine
freshly ground black pepper

1 Heat 1 tablespoon oil in a large skillet and cook bacon, onions and garlic for 4-5 minutes or until onions are soft. Transfer to a large casserole or baking dish.

2 Heat remaining oil in skillet and cook pork and lamb in batches over a high heat for 4-5 minutes or until browned on all sides. Transfer to casserole. Add sausages to skillet and cook for 4-5 minutes or until browned on all sides. Remove, cut each sausage into three and add to casserole.

3 Stir beans, tomato purée, tomatoes, sage, thyme, stock and wine into casserole and bake for 1½-2 hours or until meat is tender. Season to taste with black pepper and serve.

Serves 10

Oven temperature
300°F, 150°C

This version of the traditional dish is great for feeding a crowd. Its name comes from the special earthenware dish that was originally used to cook it in – a cassolo.

Mexican Meatloaf

Oven temperature
350°F, 180°C

To cook this meatloaf in the microwave, mix as described in the recipe, then press half the meat mixture into a lightly greased 4$^1/_2$ x 8$^1/_2$ in/11 x 21 cm microwave-safe loaf container. Top with half the shredded cheese, then cover with remaining meat mixture. Cook on MEDIUM-HIGH (70%) for 15 minutes. Drain off any liquid and stand for 10 minutes. Turn meatloaf onto a microwave-safe plate, top and cook on HIGH (100%) for 3 minutes or until cheese melts.

1 lb/500 g lean ground lamb or beef
2 tablespoons or 1 oz/30 g package taco seasoning mix
1 egg
1 cup/60 g fresh bread crumbs
1 cup/125 g shredded mature Cheddar cheese
1 cup/250 mL bottled taco sauce
1 oz/30 g corn chips

1 Place meat, taco seasoning mix, egg and bread crumbs in a bowl and mix to combine. Press half the meat mixture into a lightly greased 4$^1/_2$ x 8$^1/_2$ in/11 x 21 cm loaf pan. Top with half the shredded cheese, then cover with remaining meat mixture. Bake for 40 minutes, then drain off any liquid, cover and set aside to stand for 10 minutes.

2 Turn meatloaf onto an ovenproof plate, brush with taco sauce and top with corn chips and remaining cheese. Bake at 400°F/200°C for 10 minutes or until cheese is melted. Serve hot, warm or cold.

Serves 4

Pork Sirloin Roast

Left: Mexican Meatloaf
Above: Pork Sirloin Roast

3 lb/1.5 kg boneless pork sirloin roast (with rind and fat left on, if desired)
1 tablespoon coarse cooking salt

SPINACH STUFFING

2 tablespoons/30 g butter
4 large spinach leaves, stalks removed and leaves shredded
3 tablespoons pine nuts (pignola)
1/2 cup/30 g fresh bread crumbs
1/4 teaspoon ground nutmeg
freshly ground black pepper

CHUNKY APPLE RELISH

1 small green apple, peeled, cored and sliced
1 small pear, peeled, cored and sliced
2 teaspoons chopped dried dates
1/3 cup/90 mL apple juice
2 teaspoons honey
1 teaspoon finely grated lemon peel
pinch ground cloves

Serves 8

1 Unroll sirloin and, with a sharp knife, increase the pocket made from removing the bone, making a space for the stuffing. Score the rind with a sharp knife, cutting down into the fat under the rind.

2 To make stuffing, melt butter in a skillet and cook spinach and pine nuts (pignola) for 2-3 minutes or until spinach wilts. Remove pan from heat and stir in bread crumbs, nutmeg and black pepper to taste. Spread spinach mixture over cut flap.

3 Roll up sirloin firmly and secure with string. Place in a roasting pan, rub all over rind (if left on) with salt and bake for 20 minutes. Reduce oven temperature to 350°F/180°C and bake for 1 hour longer or until juices run clear when tested with a skewer in the meatiest part.

4 To make relish, place apple, pear, dates, apple juice, honey, lemon peel and cloves in a small saucepan, cover and bring to the boil. Reduce heat and simmer for 5 minutes or until apple is tender. Serve with pork.

Oven temperature
500°F, 250°C

The rind and fat layer can be removed from the sirloin, if desired. Omit coarse salt and roast at 350°F/180°C for the full cooking time.

Honey-glazed Ham

Oven temperature
350°F, 180°C

A glazed ham makes the perfect main dish for any buffet. It is delicious served hot, warm or cold. If serving hot, allow the ham to stand for 10 minutes before carving. If serving cold, glaze the ham the day before and then refrigerate. Cold meats are more succulent at room temperature, so remove the ham from the refrigerator 20 minutes before serving.

8 lb/4 kg cooked leg ham
whole cloves

HONEY GLAZE
1/2 cup/170 g honey
1 cup/250 mL orange juice
1 tablespoon Dijon mustard
2 teaspoons soy sauce
1 tablespoon packed brown sugar

1 Remove skin from ham. To remove skin cut a scallop pattern through the skin around the shank bone, then, starting at the broad end of the ham and using your fingers, gently ease skin away from the fat.

2 Using a sharp knife score the fat in a diamond pattern, taking care not to cut right through into the meat. Place ham in a large baking pan.

3 To make glaze, place honey, orange juice, mustard, soy sauce and brown sugar in a small saucepan and cook over a low heat, stirring, until honey and sugar melt. Brush ham with some of the glaze, then stud each diamond section with a whole clove and bake for 1 hour, brushing with remaining glaze every 20 minutes.

Serves 25

Oriental Spareribs

Oven temperature
350°C, 180°C

Eating and enjoying ribs can be messy. When serving ribs it is a good idea to supply bowls of water for washing fingers, and large napkins. At many rib restaurants the diner is supplied with a bib!

2 lb/1 kg pork spareribs, trimmed of all visible fat and cut in 6 in/15 cm lengths

ORIENTAL MARINADE
1/4 cup/60 mL hoisin sauce
1/4 cup/60 mL tomato catsup
2 tablespoons soy sauce
1/4 cup/90 g honey
2 cloves garlic, crushed
2 teaspoons grated fresh ginger
1 teaspoon chili sauce
1 teaspoon Chinese five spice powder

1 To make marinade, place hoisin sauce, catsup, soy sauce, honey, garlic, ginger, chili sauce and five spice powder in a bowl and mix to combine. Add ribs and toss to coat. Cover and refrigerate for 8 hours or overnight.

2 Remove ribs from marinade and reserve marinade. Place ribs in a single layer on a rack set over a roasting pan. Bake, basting occasionally with reserved marinade, for 40 minutes or until ribs are tender.

Serves 8

Honey-glazed Ham

Moroccan Stew

For an attractive presentation, serve this stew on a bed of saffron rice. To make saffron rice, soak a few strands of saffron in 3 tablespoons warm water and add to water when cooking rice. Instead of saffron you can use 1/4 teaspoon ground turmeric, in which case there is no need to soak it; simply add to water and rice.

1 tablespoon vegetable oil
1 lb/500 g chuck or blade steak, cut into 1 in/2.5 cm cubes
2 cups/500 mL beef stock
2 teaspoons ground cinnamon
2 tablespoons honey
1/2 teaspoon ground turmeric
1/2 teaspoon ground nutmeg
1/3 cup/60 g golden raisins
1/2 cup/60 g dried apricots, chopped
8 baby boiling onions
2 tablespoons orange juice
1/3 cup/60 g/2 oz blanched almonds
freshly ground black pepper

Serves 4

1 Heat oil in a heavy-based saucepan and cook meat over a high heat for 4-5 minutes or until browned on all sides. Stir in stock and cinnamon, bring to the boil, then reduce heat and simmer for 10 minutes, stirring to lift any sediment from base of pan.

2 Add honey, turmeric, nutmeg, raisins and apricots to pan, cover and simmer for 30 minutes.

3 Stir in onions, orange juice and almonds and simmer, uncovered, for 30 minutes longer or until meat is tender. Season to taste with black pepper.

Lamb Fillo Parcels

Oven temperature 425°F, 220°C

8 lean frenched lamb rib chops
2 cloves garlic, cut into slivers
2 teaspoons coarse grain mustard
3 oz/90 g blue cheese
1 tablespoon/15 g butter, softened
1 teaspoon port or sherry
16 sheets fillo (phyllo) pastry
1/4 cup/60 mL olive oil

VEGETABLE FILLING
1 tablespoon/15 g butter
4 spring onions, chopped
1 red pepper, finely chopped
8 button mushrooms, finely chopped
2 large lettuce leaves, shredded

1 Trim meat of all visible fat and insert a sliver of garlic between meat and bone of each chop. Cook chops under a preheated broiler for 2-4 minutes each side or until just browned but not cooked through. Spread both sides of each chop with mustard. Place cheese, butter and port or sherry in a small bowl, mix to combine and top each chop with a spoonful of mixture.

2 To make filling, melt butter in a skillet and cook spring onions, red pepper, mushrooms and lettuce for 2-3 minutes or until spring onions soften and lettuce wilts. Set aside to cool slightly.

3 Working with 2 sheets of pastry, brush between sheets with oil, fold in half, then in half again to form a square. Brush between folds with oil. Spread a little of the vegetable mixture over pastry, top with a chop, then top with more vegetable mixture. Fold pastry to enclose chop, leaving bone exposed, brush with oil and place on a baking sheet.

4 Repeat with remaining pastry, chops and vegetable mixture. Bake chops for 10 minutes or until pastry is golden brown.

Serves 4

Reduce fat intake by cutting all visible fat from meat before cooking. The more fat you trim off before cooking, the easier it is to make healthy, low-fat meat meals.

Glazed Corned Beef

3 lb/1.5 kg corned boneless brisket
2 tablespoons packed brown sugar
1 tablespoon cider vinegar
2 sprigs fresh mint
1 onion, peeled and studded with 4 whole cloves
6 black peppercorns
6 small carrots
6 small onions
3 parsnips, halved

REDCURRANT GLAZE
1/2 cup/155 g redcurrant jelly
2 tablespoons orange juice
1 tablespoon sweet sherry

1 Place brisket in a large heavy-based saucepan. Add brown sugar, vinegar, mint, clove-studded onion, peppercorns and enough water to cover meat. Cover, bring to the boil over a medium heat, then reduce heat and simmer for 1 1/4-1 1/2 hours.

2 Add carrots, onions and parsnips to pan and simmer for 40 minutes longer or until vegetables are tender.

3 To make glaze, place redcurrant jelly, orange juice and sherry in a small saucepan and cook over a low heat, stirring occasionally, until jelly melts and glaze is blended. Transfer meat to a warm serving platter and brush with glaze. Slice meat and serve with vegetables and any remaining glaze.

Serves 6

Simple and satisfying, corned beef is delicious served with creamy mashed potatoes and horseradish cream. To make horseradish cream, whip 1/2 cup/125 mL whipping cream until soft peaks form, then fold in 3 tablespoons bottled horseradish.

Moroccan Stew

Steak and Kidney Pie

Oven temperature
425°F, 220°C

A trick to remember with any meat-filled pie is to completely fill the pie dish so the pastry is supported from below and bakes without sinking.

2 lb/1 kg lean top round steak, cut into 1 in/2.5 cm cubes
6 lamb's kidneys or 1 ox kidney, cored and roughly chopped
5 tablespoons all-purpose flour
1 tablespoon vegetable oil
2 cloves garlic, crushed
2 onions, chopped
$^1/_2$ teaspoon dry mustard
2 tablespoons chopped fresh parsley
2 tablespoons Worcestershire sauce
$1^1/_2$ cups/375 mL beef stock
2 teaspoons tomato paste
1 sheet prerolled frozen puff pastry, thawed
2 tablespoons milk

1 Place steak, kidneys and flour in a plastic bag and shake to coat meat with flour. Shake off excess flour and set aside. Heat oil in a large skillet and cook meat over a high heat, stirring, until brown on all sides. Reduce heat to medium, add garlic and onions and cook for 3 minutes longer. Stir in mustard, parsley, Worcestershire sauce, stock and tomato paste, bring to simmering, cover and simmer, stirring occasionally, for $2^1/_2$ hours or until meat is tender. Remove pan from heat and set aside to cool completely.

2 Place cooled filling in a 4 cup/1 liter capacity glass or ceramic pie dish. On a lightly floured surface, roll out pastry sheet, if necessary, to 2 in/5 cm larger than pie dish. Cut off a $^1/_2$ in/1 cm strip from pastry edge. Brush rim of dish with water and press pastry strip onto rim. Brush pastry strip with water. Lift pastry top over filling and press gently to seal edges. Trim and knock back edges to make a decorative edge. Brush with milk and bake for 30 minutes or until pastry is golden and crisp.

Serves 6

Steak and Kidney Pie

Pork and Chicken Loaf

Pork and Chicken Loaf

2 tablespoons/30 g butter
1 onion, chopped
1 clove garlic, crushed
$1^1/2$ lb/750 g lean ground pork
3 tablespoons chopped fresh parsley
2 eggs
2 teaspoons canned (bottled) green peppercorns, drained
1 tablespoon dry vermouth
2 sheets prerolled frozen puff pastry
2 boned, skinned chicken breast halves, pounded flat
1 egg white, lightly beaten

Serves 6

1 Melt butter in a skillet and cook onion and garlic over a medium heat for 4-5 minutes or until onion softens. Place pork, parsley, eggs, peppercorns, vermouth and onion mixture in a bowl. Mix to combine.

2 Slightly overlap, seal then trim pastry sheets to make a 12 x 16 in/30 x 40 cm rectangle. Reserve pastry scraps. Cut a 3 in/7.5 cm square from each corner – this eliminates bulkiness when folded. Press pork mixture down center of pastry to form a rectangular shape. Top with chicken breasts and wrap up like a parcel. Cut pastry leaves from pastry scraps and use to decorate top of loaf.

3 Brush with egg white and place on a greased roasting rack set over a baking pan and bake for $1\text{-}1^1/2$ hours or until pastry is crisp and golden.

Oven temperature
350°F, 180°C

Served hot with mashed potatoes and a green vegetable, this loaf makes a hearty winter meal. Served cold with a selection of chutneys and a tossed lettuce salad, it is wonderful for a summer dinner or picnic.

Beef with Lemon Grass

2 tablespoons vegetable oil
2 onions, chopped
1 teaspoon whole allspice
1 x 2 in/5 cm cinnamon stick
1 teaspoon grated fresh ginger
2 green peppers, cut into strips
1 1/2 lb/750 g chuck steak, cut into 1 in/2.5 cm cubes
2 tablespoons chopped fresh lemon grass or 3 teaspoons dried lemon grass
2 cups/500 mL chicken stock
1 lb/500 g butternut squash or carrots, peeled and cut into 1 in/2.5 cm cubes
2 cloves garlic, crushed
freshly ground black pepper

1 Heat oil in a large heavy-based saucepan and cook onions over a medium heat for 10 minutes or until golden. Stir in allspice, cinnamon stick, ginger and green peppers and cook for 1 minute longer.

2 Add meat to pan and cook over a high heat for 4-5 minutes or until browned on all sides. Stir in lemon grass and stock, bring to the boil, then reduce heat, cover and simmer for 45 minutes.

3 Add squash or carrots to pan. Cover and simmer for 45 minutes longer or until beef and squash are tender. Remove pan from heat, stir in garlic and season to taste with black pepper.

Serves 6

Lemon grass is a tender, lemon-scented grass of the tropics. Much used in Southeast Asian cooking, it is available fresh or dried from oriental specialty shops. If you cannot obtain it, use finely grated lemon peel instead.

Sausage Ragout

12 baby potatoes, scrubbed
12 baby boiling onions
1/4 cup/60 mL soy sauce
1/2 cup/125 mL lemon juice
1 cup/250 mL beef stock
1 cup/250 mL dry white wine
3 tablespoons chopped fresh basil

HERBED SAUSAGES
1 lb/500 g lean ground beef
4 tablespoons chopped fresh parsley
4 tablespoons chopped fresh basil
3 tablespoons pine nuts (pignola)
1 tablespoon olive oil
2 cloves garlic, crushed
3 cups/185 g fresh bread crumbs
3 tablespoons grated Parmesan cheese
freshly ground black pepper
seasoned flour
oil for deep-frying

1 To make sausages, place beef, parsley, basil, pine nuts (pignola), oil, garlic, bread crumbs, Parmesan cheese and black pepper to taste in a large bowl and mix to combine. Shape mixture into twelve sausages, each 4 in/10 cm long. Roll each sausage in seasoned flour and set aside.

2 Heat oil in a large saucepan and cook sausages a few at a time until browned, but not cooked through. Remove sausages and drain on paper towels.

3 Place sausages, potatoes and onions in a large saucepan. Place soy sauce, lemon juice, stock, wine and basil in a bowl and mix to combine. Pour over sausages in saucepan, bring to the boil, then reduce heat, cover and simmer for 20 minutes or until potatoes and onions are tender.

Serves 6

For a complete meal, serve this tasty ragout with a chilled tomato salad and crusty French bread.

Coriander-filled Pork

Bean Lasagne

Bean Lasagne

Oven temperature
350°F, 180°C

12 large spinach leaves, chopped
8 oz/250 g lasagne sheets
4 oz/125 g shredded mature Cheddar cheese
2 tablespoons grated Parmesan cheese

TOMATO BEAN SAUCE
1 tablespoon olive oil
2 onions, chopped
2 cloves garlic, crushed
14 oz/440 g canned tomatoes, undrained
14 oz/440 g canned lima or butter beans, drained and puréed
14 oz/440 g canned red kidney beans, drained
1 teaspoon hot chili sauce
1 teaspoon dried oregano

1 To make sauce, heat oil in a large skillet and cook onions and garlic for 4-5 minutes or until onions are soft. Stir in tomatoes, lima or butter bean purée, red kidney beans, chili sauce and oregano. Bring to the boil, then reduce heat and simmer, uncovered, for 10 minutes or until sauce reduces and thickens. Remove sauce from heat and set aside.

2 Place a little water in a saucepan and bring to the boil, add spinach and cook for 1-2 minutes or until spinach wilts. Drain and set aside. Cook lasagne sheets in boiling water in a large saucepan following package directions. Drain.

3 Place one-third lasagne sheets in the base of a lightly greased, shallow ovenproof dish, then top with one-third of the bean sauce and half of the spinach. Repeat layers, then finish with a layer of lasagne sheets and remaining bean sauce. Sprinkle with Cheddar cheese and Parmesan cheese. Bake for 30 minutes or until lasagne is heated through and top is golden.

Serves 6

Quick Fettuccine with Scallops

1 lb/500 g fettuccine
1 tablespoon finely chopped fresh parsley

SCALLOP SAUCE
2 tablespoons/30 g butter
1 red pepper, cut into strips
2 spring onions, finely chopped
1 cup/250 mL whipping cream
1 lb/500 g frozen scallops, thawed
freshly ground black pepper

1 Cook fettuccine in boiling water in a large saucepan following package directions. Drain, set aside and keep warm.

2 To make sauce, melt butter in a large skillet and cook red pepper and spring onions for 1-2 minutes. Add cream and bring to the boil, then reduce heat and simmer for 5 minutes or until sauce reduces slightly and thickens.

3 Stir scallops into sauce and cook for 2-3 minutes or until scallops are opaque. Season to taste with black pepper. Place fettuccine in a warm serving bowl, top with sauce and sprinkle with parsley.

Serves 4

A salad of mixed lettuces refreshes the palate and is the ideal accompaniment for this rich dish.

Quick Fettuccine with Scallops

Cheesy Meatballs with Spaghetti

Cheesy Meatballs with Spaghetti

8 oz/250 g spaghetti

CHEESY MEATBALLS
1 lb/500 g lean ground beef
2 tablespoons finely chopped fresh parsley
$^{1}/_{2}$ cup/60 g grated Parmesan cheese
2 teaspoons tomato paste
1 egg, beaten

TOMATO SAUCE
1 tablespoon/15 g butter
1 onion, finely chopped
2 teaspoons dried basil
1 teaspoon dried oregano
14 oz/440 g canned tomatoes, undrained and mashed
2 tablespoons tomato paste
$^{1}/_{2}$ cup/125 mL beef stock
$^{1}/_{2}$ cup/125 mL white wine
1 teaspoon superfine sugar
freshly ground black pepper

1 To make meatballs, place beef, parsley, Parmesan cheese, tomato paste and egg in a bowl, and mix to combine. Form mixture into small balls and cook in a nonstick skillet for 4-5 minutes or until brown. Remove meatballs from pan and drain on paper towels.

2 To make sauce, melt butter in a large skillet and cook onion, basil and oregano for 2-3 minutes or until onion is soft. Stir in tomatoes, tomato paste, beef stock, wine and sugar. Bring to the boil, then reduce heat and simmer, stirring occasionally, for 30 minutes or until sauce reduces and thickens. Season to taste with black pepper. Add meatballs to sauce and cook for 5 minutes longer.

3 Cook spaghetti in boiling water in a large saucepan following package directions. Drain, place in a warm serving bowl and top with meatballs and sauce. Serve immediately.

Serves 4

What's the easiest way to eat ribbon pasta? Firstly, serve it in a shallow bowl or on a plate with a slight rim. To ensure that the pasta stays hot while you are eating it, heat the plates before serving. To eat the pasta, slip a few strands on to your fork, then twirl them against the plate, or a spoon, into a ball – the trick is to take only small forkfuls and to wind the pasta tightly so that there are no dangling strands.

Chicken, Pasta Toss

1 lb/500 g shell pasta
2 tablespoons/30 g butter
1 onion, finely chopped
1 clove garlic, crushed
8 oz/250 g cooked chicken, shredded
1/2 cup/125 mL chicken stock
6 large spinach leaves, shredded
freshly ground black pepper
2 oz/60 g pine nuts (pignola), toasted

1 Cook pasta in boiling water in a large saucepan following package directions. Drain, set aside and keep warm.

2 Melt butter in a large skillet and cook onion and garlic, stirring, over a medium heat for 3-4 minutes. Add chicken and stock, and cook for 4-5 minutes longer.

3 Add spinach and pasta to pan, season to taste with black pepper and toss to combine. Sprinkle with pine nuts (pignola) and serve immediately.

Serves 4

Chicken, Pasta Toss

This pretty pasta dish looks wonderful served with a salad of julienne carrots. To make the salad, cut 3 large carrots into strips and boil or microwave until just tender. Drain, refresh under cold running water, drain again and place in a salad bowl. Place 2 tablespoons lemon juice, 1 tablespoon Dijon mustard, 4 tablespoons olive oil and 1 tablespoon snipped fresh chives in a screwtop jar and shake to combine. Spoon over carrots and toss to combine. Cover and chill for 1 hour or until required.

Beef Lasagne

Oven temperature
375°F, 190°C

As an accompaniment to this substantial lasagne choose something light, such as a tomato and herb salad.

9 sheets microwavable (no precooking required) lasagne
1/2 cup/60 g shredded mature Cheddar cheese
2 tablespoons grated Parmesan cheese

MEAT SAUCE
2 teaspoons olive oil
1 onion, chopped
2 cloves garlic, crushed
2 slices bacon, chopped
4 oz/125 g button mushrooms, sliced
1 lb/500 g lean ground beef
14 oz/440 g canned tomatoes, undrained and mashed
1/2 cup/125 mL red wine
1/2 teaspoon dried basil
1/2 teaspoon dried oregano
1 teaspoon sugar

SPINACH CHEESE SAUCE
2 tablespoons/30 g butter
2 tablespoons all-purpose flour
1 cup/250 mL milk
1/2 cup/125 mL light cream (half and half)
1/2 cup/60 g shredded mature Cheddar cheese
8 oz/250 g frozen spinach, thawed and drained
freshly ground black pepper

1 To make Meat Sauce, heat oil in a large skillet and cook onion, garlic, bacon and mushrooms over a medium heat for 4-5 minutes or until onion is soft.

2 Add beef to pan and cook, stirring to break up meat, for 4-5 minutes or until meat is brown. Combine tomatoes, wine, basil, oregano and sugar, and pour into pan with meat mixture. Bring to the boil, then reduce heat, cover and simmer for 35 minutes or until sauce thickens.

3 To make Spinach Cheese Sauce, melt butter in a saucepan and cook flour for 1-2 minutes. Remove pan from heat and stir in milk and cream. Cook, stirring constantly, over a medium heat for 4-5 minutes or until sauce boils and thickens. Remove pan from heat and stir in cheese and spinach. Season to taste with black pepper.

4 To assemble lasagne, spread one-third of the Spinach Cheese Sauce over base of a lightly greased, shallow 7 x 11 in/ 18 x 28 cm ovenproof dish. Top with three lasagne sheets, spread half the Meat Sauce over, then another third of the Spinach Cheese Sauce. Top with another three lasagne sheets and remaining Meat Sauce. Place remaining lasagne sheets over Meat Sauce and top with remaining Spinach Cheese Sauce.

5 Combine Cheddar and Parmesan cheese and sprinkle over lasagne and bake for 40 minutes or until top is golden.

Serves 6

Beef Lasagne

Tortellini with Red Pepper Sauce

1 lb/500 g tortellini

RED PEPPER SAUCE
1 tablespoon vegetable oil
1 onion, chopped
14 oz/440 g canned sweet red peppers, drained and chopped
1 cup/250 mL water
1 tablespoon honey
1 tablespoon chopped fresh oregano
freshly ground black pepper

1 Cook tortellini in boiling water in a large saucepan, following package directions. Drain, set aside and keep warm.

2 To make sauce, heat oil in a small skillet and cook onion, stirring, for 3 minutes or until onion is soft. Place red peppers, water, honey, oregano and onion in a food processor or blender and process to make a smooth sauce.

3 Pour pepper sauce into a saucepan and heat over a medium heat for 4-5 minutes or until sauce is simmering. Season to taste with black pepper. Spoon sauce over tortellini and toss to combine.

Serves 4

Canned sweet red peppers are available from Continental delicatessens and some supermarkets. They are sometimes called pimentos.
You may wish to use fresh red peppers instead of the canned ones. You will require 4 large peppers for this recipe and they need to be roasted and the skin removed before making the sauce.

Rice-filled Chicken

Oven temperature
350°F, 180°C

To test when a bird is cooked, place a skewer into the thickest part of the thigh and when the skewer is removed the juices should run clear. If the juices are tinged pink, return bird to the oven and cook for 15 minutes longer, then test again. On completion of cooking, allow whole birds to stand in a warm place for 10-20 minutes before carving. This tenderizes the meat by allowing the juices to settle into the flesh.

1 x 3 lb/1.5 kg chicken, cleaned
4 slices bacon, chopped
4 spring onions, chopped
2 teaspoons curry powder
$^3/_4$ cup/170 g long grain rice, cooked
1 cup/60 g fresh bread crumbs
1 tablespoon olive oil

MUSHROOM SAUCE
2 tablespoons/30 g butter
1 onion, chopped
1 green pepper, chopped
4 oz/125 g mushrooms, sliced
14 oz/440 g canned tomatoes, undrained and mashed
2 tablespoons tomato paste
$^1/_4$ cup/60 mL red wine
1 tablespoon sugar
$^1/_2$ cup/125 mL water
freshly ground black pepper

Serves 4

1 Using paper towels, pat chicken dry inside and out. Cook bacon, spring onions and curry powder in a skillet over a medium heat for 4-5 minutes or until bacon is crisp. Remove pan from heat and stir in rice and bread crumbs.

2 Fill cavity of chicken with rice mixture and secure opening with metal or bamboo skewers. Tuck wings under body of chicken and tie legs together. Place bird breast side up in a baking pan. Brush with oil and bake, basting frequently with pan juices, for $1^1/_2$ hours or until bird is cooked.

3 To make sauce, melt butter in a saucepan and cook onion, green pepper and mushrooms for 2-3 minutes. Stir in tomatoes, tomato paste, wine, sugar, water and black pepper to taste. Cook, stirring constantly, over a medium heat for 10-15 minutes or until sauce is reduced by a quarter. Serve sauce with chicken.

Chicken with Corn

Oven temperature
350°F, 180°C

Serve this rich cumin-flavored chicken and corn on a bed of boiled rice and accompany with a green vegetable such as beans, asparagus or spinach.

1 tablespoon olive oil
2 onions, chopped
2 teaspoons ground cumin
4 chicken thighs
4 chicken drumsticks
1 cup/250 mL dry white wine
1 cup/250 mL chicken stock
1 cup/250 mL whipping cream
10 oz/315 g canned sweet corn kernels, drained

Serves 4

1 Heat oil in a large skillet and cook onions and cumin over a medium heat for 4-5 minutes or until onions are soft. Add chicken and cook for 8-10 minutes longer or until brown on all sides. Transfer onions and chicken to a casserole dish.

2 Drain fat from pan and stir in wine. Bring to the boil, stirring and scraping bits from base of pan. Boil for 4-5 minutes or until reduced by half.

3 Stir stock, cream and corn into wine and cook for 5 minutes longer. Pour wine mixture over chicken, cover and bake for 45-60 minutes or until chicken is cooked.

Rice-filled Chicken

Almond Chicken Rolls

4 boned, skinned chicken breast halves
vegetable oil for deep-frying

BREAD CRUMB COATING
2 eggs
$^1/_3$ cup/90 mL milk
$^1/_2$ cup/60 g seasoned flour
2 cups/125 g fresh bread crumbs

HERB BUTTER
$^3/_4$ cup/1$^1/_2$ sticks/185 g butter, softened
$^1/_3$ cup/60 g almonds, chopped
2 teaspoons Dijon mustard
1 tablespoon chopped fresh parsley
1 tablespoon snipped fresh chives
freshly ground black pepper

Do not allow the oil to become too hot when cooking these rolls or the coating will brown before the chicken is cooked.

1 To make Herb Butter, place butter, almonds, mustard, parsley, chives and black pepper to taste in a bowl and mix to combine. Divide butter into four portions and shape into rolls 4 in/10 cm long. Wrap rolls in plastic wrap and refrigerate until firm.

2 Place breasts between two sheets of plastic wrap and pound, using a rolling pin, to flatten. Take care not to make holes in the chicken or the butter will run out during cooking.

3 Place a butter roll in the center of each chicken breast. Fold the shorter ends into the center, then roll up to fully encase the butter. Secure rolls with toothpicks.

4 To coat, place eggs and milk in a small bowl and beat to combine. Transfer to a shallow dish. Place flour and bread crumbs on separate plates. Coat chicken rolls with flour, then dip in egg mixture and roll in bread crumbs. Repeat egg and bread crumb steps. Place rolls on a plate, cover with plastic wrap and refrigerate for 1 hour.

5 Heat oil in a large saucepan and cook chicken rolls for 5-8 minutes or until golden and cooked through.

Serves 4

Almond Chicken Rolls

Chicken Bean Bake

1 slice bacon, chopped
3 lb/1.5 kg chicken pieces, skin removed
2 onions, chopped
1 clove garlic, crushed
1/2 cup/125 mL chicken stock
1/3 cup/90 mL white wine
1 teaspoon dried mixed herbs
1 teaspoon sugar
14 oz/440 g canned tomatoes, undrained and mashed
10 oz/315 g canned lima or butter beans, drained

1 Cook bacon in a skillet, over a medium heat for 2-3 minutes or until crisp. Remove bacon from pan and drain on paper towels.

2 Cook chicken in skillet for 5-8 minutes or until brown on all sides. Remove chicken from pan and place in a casserole.

3 Add onions and garlic to pan and cook for 2-3 minutes or until onion is soft. Scatter onion mixture and bacon over chicken pieces.

4 Stir stock, wine, herbs, sugar and tomatoes into pan and bring to the boil over a medium heat. Cook, stirring occasionally, until mixture reduces and thickens. Stir in beans and pour over chicken. Cover and bake for 45-60 minutes or until chicken is cooked.

Serves 6

Oven temperature
400°F, 200°C

When cooking poultry pieces, remember that the breast – the white meat – cooks more quickly than the legs and thighs – the dark meat. Cooking the leg and thigh portions for 10 minutes before adding the breast portions will give you evenly cooked poultry pieces.

Chicken Bean Bake

Pimento Chicken Pie

Oven temperature
350°F, 180°C

A chicken pie with a difference. The corn meal pastry has a deliciously different texture and the filling is like no other you have tasted. For a complete meal, serve with a salad of mixed lettuces, tomatoes and olives tossed in a light vinaigrette dressing.

CORN MEAL PASTRY

$1\frac{1}{2}$ cups/185 g all-purpose flour
$\frac{1}{2}$ cup/60 g corn meal
$\frac{1}{2}$ cup/1 stick/125 g butter, cut into pieces
1 egg, lightly beaten
$\frac{1}{2}$ cup/125 mL water

CHICKEN PIMENTO FILLING

1 tablespoon olive oil
1 lb/500 g frozen spinach, thawed
2 cloves garlic, crushed
1 oz/30 g pine nuts (pignola)
5 slices prosciutto or ham, chopped
3 boned, skinned chicken breast halves, poached and chopped
2 pieces canned pimento or $\frac{1}{2}$ red pepper, cut into strips
3 eggs, lightly beaten
1 cup/250 mL whipping cream
freshly ground black pepper

1 To make pastry, place flour, corn meal and butter in a food processor and process until mixture resembles fine bread crumbs. With machine running, add egg, then water a tablespoon at a time until mixture forms a ball. Turn dough onto a lightly floured surface and knead lightly. Wrap in plastic wrap and refrigerate for 30 minutes.

2 To make filling, heat oil in a large skillet and cook spinach, garlic, pine nuts (pignola) and prosciutto or ham over a medium heat for 4-5 minutes or until pine nuts (pignola) are golden. Transfer spinach mixture to a bowl and set aside to cool completely. Add chicken, pimento or red pepper, eggs and cream, and mix to combine.

3 Roll out two-thirds of the dough on a lightly floured surface and line the base and sides of a lightly greased, deep 9 in/23 cm pie or quiche dish. Trim edges using a sharp knife. Spoon filling into dish. On a lightly floured surface, roll out remaining pastry large enough to cover pie. Brush edge of pastry with water and cover with pastry top. Press edges together to seal, then trim and make a decorative edge using fingertips. Make two slits in top of pie to allow steam to escape. Bake for 45 minutes or until pastry is golden.

Serves 8

Pimento Chicken Pie

Chicken Roll Casserole

6 boned, skinned chicken breast halves
3 slices bacon
1 tablespoon chopped fresh parsley
$^{1}/_{4}$ cup/$^{1}/_{2}$ stick/60 g butter
2 onions, chopped
2 carrots, shredded
8 large spinach leaves
freshly ground black pepper
3 potatoes, cooked
$^{1}/_{2}$ cup/125 mL water

1 Place breasts between two sheets of plastic food wrap and pound, using a rolling pin, to flatten. Remove rind from bacon and cut each slice in half. Place a piece of bacon on each chicken breast and sprinkle with parsley. Fold the shorter ends into the center, then roll up and secure rolls with toothpicks.

2 Melt half the butter in a large skillet and cook chicken rolls for 8-10 minutes or until brown on all sides. Remove rolls from pan and set aside.

3 Melt remaining butter in skillet and cook onions and carrots, stirring, for 5 minutes or until onions are soft. Add spinach and cook, stirring, for 2-3 minutes longer or until spinach is wilted. Season to taste with black pepper.

4 Cut potatoes into thick slices and place in the base of a casserole dish. Top with vegetable mixture, then chicken rolls. Pour water over, cover and bake for 35-40 minutes or until chicken rolls are cooked.

Serves 6

Oven temperature
350°F, 180°C

Chicken rolls filled with bacon and parsley make a complete meal when teamed with vegetables and cooked in a casserole. Serve with crusty bread rolls or garlic bread.

Chicken Roll Casserole

Chicken Pot Pie

Oven temperature
400°F, 200°C

A delicious herb topping is an imaginative alternative to potatoes in this cobbler-style recipe. Serve with a green vegetable, such as beans, spinach or cabbage, for a complete meal.

1/4 cup/1/2 stick/60 g butter
1 large onion, chopped
4 boned, skinned chicken breast halves, cut into 3/4 in/2 cm cubes
2 potatoes, cut into 1/2 in/1 cm cubes
2 large carrots, cut into 1/2 in/1 cm cubes
1/4 cup/30 g all-purpose flour
1 cup/250 mL dry white wine
3 cups/750 mL chicken stock
1 cup/250 mL whipping cream
2 tablespoons tomato paste

HERBED BISCUIT TOPPING

2 cups/250 g self-rising flour, sifted
1 teaspoon dried mixed herbs
1/4 cup/30 g grated fresh Parmesan cheese
2 tablespoons/30 g butter, chopped
1 cup/250 mL milk

1 Melt butter in a large skillet and cook onion, stirring, over a medium heat for 3-4 minutes or until onion is soft. Add chicken and cook, stirring, for 3 minutes longer.

2 Add potatoes and carrots and cook, stirring, for 8-10 minutes. Stir in flour, then wine, stock, cream and tomato paste, and bring to simmering. Simmer for 10 minutes then transfer mixture to a casserole dish.

3 To make topping, place flour, herbs, Parmesan cheese and butter in a food processor and process to combine. With machine running, add milk and process to form a sticky dough. Turn dough onto a lightly floured surface and knead until smooth. Press dough out to 3/4 in/2 cm thick and, using a biscuit cutter, cut out rounds and place on top of casserole.

4 Bake for 20-25 minutes or until topping is cooked and golden, and casserole is hot.

Serves 4

Chicken Pot Pie

Herbed Squab

Herbed Squab

4 x 12-14 oz/375-440 g squab, ready-to-cook
4 sprigs fresh thyme
4 slices bacon, rind removed

HERB BUTTER MARINADE
1 tablespoon dried mixed herbs
1/3 cup/90 g butter, melted
1/4 cup/60 mL vegetable oil

Serves 4

1 To make marinade, place herbs, butter and oil in a small bowl and mix to combine.

2 Place a sprig of thyme in cavity of each bird. Tuck wings under and tie legs together. Wrap a bacon slice around each bird and secure with a toothpick. Place birds breast side up in a baking dish, brush with marinade and bake, basting frequently with marinade, for 30-35 minutes or until cooked.

Oven temperature
350°F, 180°C

Delicious served with a tossed salad of mixed lettuce and fresh herbs and crusty wholewheat rolls.

Redcurrant Duck

Sautéed duck breasts with a redcurrant sauce make an elegant main course. Serve with asparagus, a sauté of leek strips and new potatoes.

2 tablespoons olive oil
8 duck breasts, with skin
1/4 cup/60 mL fresh lime or lemon juice
2 tablespoons honey
1/2 cup/170 g redcurrant jelly
4 oz/125 g fresh or frozen redcurrants

1 Heat oil in a large skillet and cook duck breasts for 7-8 minutes each side or until golden and cooked to your liking. Remove from pan, set aside and keep warm.

2 Drain fat from pan and add lime or lemon juice, honey and redcurrant jelly. Bring to the boil over a medium heat, stirring to lift sediment from base of pan. Reduce heat and simmer for 3-4 minutes or until mixture reduces and thickens slightly. Stir in redcurrants and cook, stirring, for 1 minute longer. Serve sauce with duck.

Serves 4

Chickpea Ragout

Chickpeas (garbanzo beans) take 45-60 minutes to cook. The cooking time can vary depending on the quality and age of the chickpeas and their place of origin. This recipe could be made using canned chickpeas. If using canned chickpeas, heat oil in a large skillet and cook onion, turmeric, chicken and garlic, stirring, for 4-5 minutes. Transfer chicken mixture to a saucepan and stir in 2 tablespoons lemon juice, 1 cup/250 mL stock (the remaining lemon juice and stock will not be used in this version of the recipe) and chickpeas. Bring to simmering and simmer for 15-20 minutes or until hot. Just prior to serving, sprinkle with almonds and parsley.

1/4 cup/60 mL olive oil
1 onion, chopped
1 teaspoon ground turmeric
1 x 3 lb/1.5 kg chicken, cut into 6 pieces
7 oz/220 g chickpeas (garbanzo beans), soaked overnight, drained
2 cups/500 mL chicken stock
1/4 cup/60 mL fresh lemon juice
3 cloves garlic, crushed
1/4 cup/30 g blanched almonds, toasted
1 tablespoon chopped fresh parsley

1 Heat oil in a large skillet and cook onion and turmeric, stirring, over a medium heat for 3 minutes or until onion is soft. Add chicken pieces and cook for 4 minutes each side or until golden. Remove chicken pieces from pan and set aside.

2 Add chickpeas, stock, lemon juice and garlic to pan, bring to the boil, then reduce heat and simmer for 40 minutes. Return chicken to pan and simmer for 20 minutes longer or until chicken and chickpeas are tender. Just prior to serving, sprinkle with almonds and parsley.

Serves 4

*Redcurrant Duck,
Chickpea Ragout*

Trout wrapped in Prosciutto

Oven temperature
350°F, 180°C

This simple way of preparing and cooking trout results in a deliciously fragrant fish which is moist and tender.

4 x 9 oz/280 g trout, cleaned and scaled
1 tablespoon olive oil
8 long slices prosciutto or lean ham
4 sprigs fresh thyme or rosemary

THYME MARINADE
1/2 cup/125 mL olive oil
1/4 cup/60 mL lemon juice
2 cloves garlic, crushed
1 tablespoon chopped fresh thyme or 1 teaspoon dried thyme
freshly ground black pepper

1 To make marinade, place oil, lemon juice, garlic, thyme and black pepper to taste in a small bowl and whisk to combine.

2 Place trout in a shallow glass, ceramic or stainless steel dish, pour marinade over, cover and refrigerate for 2 hours.

3 Cut four pieces of nonstick parchment paper large enough to enclose each trout. Place 2 slices of prosciutto or ham side by side on each sheet of paper. Remove trout from marinade and place on prosciutto or ham. Place a sprig of thyme or rosemary in the cavity of each trout and wrap prosciutto or ham around trout. Spoon over remaining marinade and fold parchment paper around trout to enclose. Seal edges by rolling together tightly.

4 Place parcels on a baking sheet and bake for 20-25 minutes or until flesh flakes when tested with a fork.

Serves 4

Rosemary Mackerel Steaks

Mackerel is an oily fish and so is high in Omega-3 fatty acids, making it ideal for anyone on a cholesterol-lowering diet. Omega-3 helps to lower blood pressure and reduce the fatty build-up on blood vessel walls. It has also been shown to reduce the tendency for the blood to clot and so lessens its 'stickiness'.

1 tablespoon olive oil
2 cloves garlic, crushed
4 x 5 oz/155 g mackerel steaks or thick fillets
1/4 cup/60 mL lemon juice
2 teaspoons fresh rosemary leaves or 1/2 teaspoon dried rosemary
freshly ground black pepper

1 Heat oil in a large nonstick skillet and cook garlic for 1 minute. Add steaks or fillets and cook for 3-4 minutes each side or until fish is browned.

2 Pour lemon juice over fish, sprinkle with rosemary and season to taste with black pepper. Cover and simmer for 5-8 minutes or until fish flakes when tested with a fork. Serve immediately.

Serves 4

Trout wrapped in Prosciutto,
Rosemary Mackerel Steaks,
Fish with Rice Stuffing

Whole Fish baked in Paper

Oven temperature
350°F, 180°C

Cooking fish in paper prevents it from drying out and nearly all types of fish are suitable to cook this way. The fish is cooked when the paper browns and puffs up. The best part of cooking fish in this way is when you open the parcel and release the rich aroma that has formed during cooking. The French call this method of cooking *en papillote*.

1 tablespoon olive oil
4 large zucchini, cut into strips
2 red peppers, cut into strips
peel from 1/2 lemon, cut into strips
4 small whole fish, such as bream, sea perch, snapper or pompano, cleaned and scaled
2 tablespoons lemon juice

1 Heat oil in a large skillet and stir-fry zucchini, red peppers and lemon peel over a medium heat for 2-3 minutes. Remove pan from heat.

2 Cut four pieces of nonstick parchment paper large enough to enclose each fish. Divide vegetable mixture between pieces of paper and top each with a fish. Sprinkle with lemon juice and fold parchment paper around fish to enclose. Seal edges by rolling together tightly. Bake for 30 minutes or until flesh flakes when tested with a fork.

Serves 4

Left: Whole Fish baked in Paper
Below: Pan-fried Fish Fillets

Pan-fried Fish Fillets

8 x 2 oz/60 g or
4 x 4 oz/125 g firm white fish fillets
3/4 cup/90 g all-purpose flour
2 eggs, beaten
1 cup/125 g dry bread crumbs
1/4 cup/1/2 stick/60 g butter

1 Dredge fillets in flour, then dip in egg and roll in bread crumbs. Place fillets on a plate lined with plastic wrap and refrigerate for 15 minutes or until ready to cook.

2 Melt butter in a large skillet and cook fillets over a medium heat for 3-5 minutes each side or until flesh flakes when tested with a fork. Serve immediately.

Serves 4

These fillets are delicious served with a bean salad made of cooked green beans, cooked chickpeas, cherry tomatoes, basil and thin strips of orange peel, tossed in a citrus dressing. To make the dressing, place 3 tablespoons olive oil, 1 crushed clove garlic, 1 tablespoon lime juice, 1 tablespoon lemon juice and 3 tablespoons orange juice in a screwtop jar and shake well to combine.

Seafood Lasagne

Oven temperature
350°F, 180°C

2 tablespoons olive oil
1 leek, white part only, sliced
14 oz/440 g canned tomatoes, undrained and mashed
2 tablespoons tomato paste
1 lb/500 g uncooked shrimp, shelled, deveined and chopped
8 oz/250 g firm white fish fillets, cut into pieces
freshly ground black pepper
15 spinach lasagne sheets
3/4 cup/90 g shredded mozzarella cheese

1 Heat oil in a large skillet and cook leek over a medium heat for 5 minutes or until it softens. Stir in tomatoes and tomato paste and bring to the boil. Reduce heat and simmer, uncovered, for 15 minutes or until sauce reduces and thickens slightly.

2 Add shrimp and fish, cover and cook for 3-4 minutes longer. Season to taste with black pepper.

3 Cook lasagne in boiling water in a large saucepan following package directions. Drain and place in a bowl of cold water.

4 Just prior to assembling, drain lasagne sheets. Spread one-third of the sauce over the base of a deep-sided ovenproof dish and top with half the lasagne sheets. Repeat layers, ending with a layer of sauce. Sprinkle with cheese and bake for 40 minutes.

Serves 6

Lasagne is a great dish when you need to feed a crowd. This recipe can easily be increased to serve 8; simply use a slightly larger dish and a little more seafood. Accompany with a tossed green salad or a sauté of mixed vegetables for a complete meal.

Seafood Lasagne

Fish and Vegetable Ragout

4 baby yellow squash or 2 zucchini, sliced
1 small head broccoli, broken into florets
2 tablespoons olive oil
1 lb/500 g firm white fish fillets, cut into large pieces
1 onion, sliced
1/2 red pepper, cut into strips
1/4 cup/1/2 stick/60 g butter
1/2 cup/125 mL dry white wine
1/2 cup/125 g dairy sour cream
freshly ground black pepper

1 Boil, steam or microwave squash or zucchini and broccoli separately until just tender. Drain and refresh under cold running water.

2 Heat oil in a large skillet and cook fish over a medium heat for 1 minute each side. Remove fish from pan and set aside. Add onion and red pepper to pan and cook for 2 minutes. Remove onion mixture from pan and set aside.

3 Add butter, wine, sour cream and black pepper to taste to pan, bring to the boil and cook, stirring, for 4-5 minutes or until mixture is reduced by one-third. Strain sauce and return to a clean pan.

4 Stir squash or zucchini, broccoli, fish and onion mixture into sauce and cook, stirring gently, for 3-4 minutes or until fish is cooked.

Serves 4

Any firm white fish fillets can be used to make this tasty ragout. You might like to use other vegetables, depending on what is in season. Carrots, parsnips, leeks and green pepper are good choices for a winter dish.

Fish with Rice Stuffing

1 x 3 lb/1.5 kg whole fish, such as snapper or bream, cleaned and skin scored
1/2 cup/125 mL dry white wine

LEEK AND RICE STUFFING

1 cup/185 g rice
2 tablespoons olive oil
2 leeks, sliced
2 cloves garlic, crushed
3 tablespoons pine nuts (pignola)
4 tablespoons golden raisins
1 stalk celery, chopped
3 tablespoons chopped fresh parsley
1 teaspoon lemon juice
1 teaspoon finely grated lemon peel
freshly ground black pepper

1 To make stuffing, cook rice following packet directions, then set aside. Heat oil in a large skillet and cook leeks and garlic for 3-4 minutes or until leeks are soft. Remove pan from heat and stir in rice, pine nuts (pignola), raisins, celery, parsley, lemon juice, lemon peel and black pepper to taste.

2 Fill cavity of fish with stuffing, close cavity and secure with wooden skewers or toothpicks. Place fish in a lightly greased, shallow baking dish. Pour wine over fish and bake for 35-40 minutes or until fish is cooked. Baste 3-4 times during cooking.

3 Place fish on a serving platter, cover, set aside and keep warm. Pour juices from baking dish into a small saucepan, bring to the boil and boil for 4-5 minutes or until juices are reduced by half. Spoon sauce over fish and serve immediately.

Serves 4

Oven temperature
350°F, 180°C

Whole fish cooks well in the microwave – but remember the eyes should be removed before cooking as they can explode.
To cook this dish in the microwave, prepare fish and stuffing as described in the recipe, then place in a shallow microwave-safe dish, pour over wine, cover and cook on MEDIUM-HIGH (70%), allowing 5-6 minutes per 1 lb/500 g of fish.

Salmon Mornay

Oven temperature
350°F, 180°C,

Fish can be a good source of bone-building calcium, an essential mineral mainly derived from milk. The edible bones in canned salmon and of tiny fish such as sardines can be consumed with the flesh and provide substantial amounts of calcium.

1/2 cup/100 g rice
1 onion, chopped
1 egg, beaten
1 tablespoon/15 g butter, melted
14 oz/440 g canned pink salmon, drained, liquid reserved and flesh flaked
1/4 cup/15 g fresh bread crumbs
1/4 cup/30 g shredded mature Cheddar cheese

CURRY SAUCE
2 cups/500 mL milk
1/4 cup/30 g cornstarch
1 teaspoon curry powder
1 teaspoon dry mustard
1 teaspoon paprika
2 tablespoons chopped fresh parsley
1 tablespoon lemon juice
1 egg, beaten
1/4 cup/30 g shredded mature Cheddar cheese
freshly ground black pepper

1 Cook rice following package directions. Place rice, onion, egg and melted butter in a bowl and mix to combine. Spread rice mixture over the base of a 7 x 11 in/18 x 28 cm ovenproof dish. Top rice mixture with salmon.

2 To make sauce, place milk, cornstarch, curry powder, mustard and paprika in a saucepan and mix well to combine. Cook sauce over a medium heat, stirring constantly, for 5-6 minutes or until sauce boils and thickens. Stir in reserved salmon liquid, parsley, lemon juice, egg, cheese and black pepper to taste. Pour sauce over salmon.

3 Combine bread crumbs and cheese and sprinkle over sauce. Bake for 40 minutes or until heated through and top is golden.

Serves 4

Barbecued Skewered Shrimp

When storing shrimp, leave them in their shell. The shell acts as a natural insulator and helps retain moisture and flavor. Cooked shrimp should be stored in the refrigerator in an airtight container or plastic bag for no longer than 3 days. Uncooked shrimp are best stored in water in an airtight container for up to 3 days. The water prevents oxidation.

1 lb/500 g large uncooked shrimp, shelled and deveined, tails left intact
2 teaspoons sesame oil
1 tablespoon soy sauce
1 tablespoon vegetable oil
1 teaspoon honey
1 clove garlic, crushed
freshly ground black pepper

1 Thread shrimp onto oiled bamboo skewers.

2 Place sesame oil, soy sauce, vegetable oil, honey, garlic and black pepper to taste in a small bowl and whisk to combine. Brush shrimp with oil mixture and cook under a preheated broiler or on a preheated barbecue grill, brushing frequently with oil mixture, for 3-4 minutes each side or until shrimp change color and are cooked.

Serves 4

Salmon Mornay,
Barbecued Skewered Shrimp

Quick Meals

If you are looking for nutritious meals that take next to no time to prepare and cook, then this is the chapter for you. Most of these dishes need only crusty bread and a salad to make a complete meal, while others are meals in themselves.

Chili Con Carne

Chili Con Carne

2 tablespoons vegetable oil
2 onions, chopped
2 cloves garlic, crushed
1/4 teaspoon chili powder
1 lb/500 g lean ground beef
1/4 cup/60 g tomato paste
1/4 cup/60 mL red wine
14 oz/440 g canned tomatoes, undrained and mashed
10 oz/315 g canned red kidney beans, drained and rinsed
freshly ground black pepper
1 cup/125 g shredded mature Cheddar cheese
1/2 cup/125 g dairy sour cream

1 Heat oil in a large skillet and cook onions, garlic and chili powder over a medium heat for 2 minutes.

2 Add beef and cook for 5 minutes longer. Stir in tomato paste, wine, tomatoes and beans, bring to simmering and simmer for 10 minutes. Season to taste with black pepper. Serve topped with shredded cheese and sour cream.

Serves 4

An all-time favorite, you can make Chili Con Carne as hot or as mild as you like, simply by adjusting the amount of chili powder that you use. For a complete meal, serve with a green salad of mixed lettuce and fresh herbs.

Beef Patties with Goat's Cheese

1 lb/500 g lean ground beef
1 egg, lightly beaten
3 tablespoons fresh bread crumbs
freshly ground black pepper
1 tomato, cut into four thick slices
3 1/2 oz/100 g goat's cheese, sliced
1 tablespoon snipped fresh chives

1 Place beef, egg, bread crumbs and black pepper to taste in a bowl and mix to combine. Divide mixture into four portions and shape into patties about 1/2 in/1 cm thick. Place patties on a plate lined with plastic wrap, cover and refrigerate for 15 minutes.

2 Cook patties under a preheated broiler for 3-4 minutes each side or until cooked to your liking. Top each pattie with a tomato slice and a cheese slice and cook under broiler for 2-3 minutes longer or until cheese melts. Sprinkle with chives and serve immediately.

Serves 4

These patties are also delicious served on toasted wholewheat rolls with lettuce and chutney.

Chili Burgers

1 lb/500 g lean ground beef
1 onion, finely chopped
freshly ground black pepper
2 tablespoons vegetable oil
4 sesame seed buns, split and toasted
4 large lettuce leaves, shredded
4 slices Gruyère cheese
1 onion, thinly sliced into rings

CHILI SAUCE
2 tablespoons olive oil
1 onion, finely chopped
2 cloves garlic, crushed
14 oz/440 g canned tomatoes, undrained and mashed
1 teaspoon chili paste (sambal oelek)
1 tablespoon chili relish
1/2 teaspoon cumin seeds

Serves 4

1 To make sauce, heat oil in a saucepan and cook onion and garlic over a medium heat for 5 minutes. Stir in tomatoes, chili paste (sambal oelek), chili relish and cumin seeds, bring to simmering and simmer, stirring occasionally, for 10 minutes or until sauce thickens and reduces.

2 Place beef, chopped onion and black pepper to taste in a bowl and mix to combine. Divide meat mixture into four portions and shape each into a 4 in/10 cm round pattie. Heat oil in a large skillet and cook patties over a medium heat for 4-5 minutes each side or until cooked to your liking.

3 To assemble burgers, top bottom half of each bun with lettuce, a meat pattie, a slice of cheese, some sauce, a few onion rings and, finally, top half of bun. Serve immediately.

Homemade burgers make a nutritious meal when teamed with a tossed green salad.

Chili Burgers

Beef Stroganoff

Beef Stroganoff

1 tablespoon vegetable oil
$1\frac{1}{2}$ lb/750 g rib eye (Delmonico) steak, cut into strips
2 onions, thinly sliced
2 cloves garlic, crushed
1 cup/250 mL beef stock
2 tablespoons tomato paste
1 tablespoon cornstarch blended with $\frac{1}{4}$ cup/60 mL water
8 oz/250 g mushrooms, sliced
freshly ground black pepper
$\frac{1}{4}$ cup/125 g dairy sour cream

Serves 6

1 Heat oil in a large skillet and cook steak in batches over a high heat for 3-4 minutes. Remove, set aside and keep warm.

2 Add onions and garlic to pan and cook over a medium heat for 5 minutes or until onions are soft. Stir in stock, tomato paste and cornstarch mixture and cook, stirring constantly, for 3-4 minutes or until sauce thickens. Add mushrooms and black pepper to taste and cook for 5 minutes longer. Remove pan from heat and stir in sour cream. Return beef to pan and toss to coat with sauce.

Try low-fat plain yogurt instead of sour cream in recipes such as this one. Stir it through at the end of cooking and do not allow to boil or the yogurt becomes grainy.

Deviled Bacon Skewers

Perfect for a special breakfast or brunch or just as a light meal, these kabobs take only minutes to prepare. Depending on what time of day you serve them, they are delicious with toasted English muffins, crusty French bread or a fresh tomato salad.

8 slices bacon
16 button mushrooms
16 cherry tomatoes
4 tablespoons fruit chutney
2 teaspoons curry powder

1 Thread bacon, mushrooms and tomatoes onto lightly oiled bamboo skewers. Thread bacon in a weaving fashion, inserting mushrooms and tomatoes, alternately, as you go.

2 Place chutney and curry powder in a small saucepan and cook over a low heat for 4-5 minutes. Brush kabobs with chutney mixture and cook under a preheated broiler for 4-5 minutes or until bacon is cooked.

Makes 8 kabobs

Bacon Omelet

An omelet is the perfect meal for people on the run. Served with a wholewheat roll and a piece of fruit for dessert, it is a quick and nutritious meal.

2 eggs
2 teaspoons water
freshly ground black pepper
1 tablespoon/15 g butter

BACON FILLING
1 slice bacon, chopped
2 tablespoons shredded Gruyère cheese

1 To make filling, cook bacon in a small skillet over a medium heat for 3-4 minutes or until crisp. Drain, place in a small bowl, add cheese and black pepper to taste. Mix to combine and set aside.

2 Place eggs, water and black pepper to taste in a small bowl and whisk to combine.

3 Heat an omelet pan over a medium heat until hot. Add butter, tipping the pan so the base is completely coated. Heat until the butter is foaming, but not browned, then add the egg mixture. As it sets use a palette knife or fork to gently draw up the edge of the omelet until no liquid remains and the omelet is lightly set.

4 Top omelet with filling, fold and slip onto serving plate. Serve immediately.

Serves 1

Deviled Bacon Skewers,
Bacon Omelet

*Pasta Shells with Anchovy Sauce,
Macaroni with Tomato Sauce*

Pasta Shells with Anchovy Sauce

1 lb/500 g small shell pasta
1/2 cup/60 g grated fresh Parmesan cheese

ANCHOVY SAUCE
2 tablespoons olive oil
3 onions, chopped
1 clove garlic, crushed
1/2 cup/125 mL dry white wine
8 canned anchovies
1 tablespoon chopped fresh rosemary leaves or 1 teaspoon dried rosemary
1 cup/250 mL beef or chicken stock
1 fresh red chili, seeded and cut into rings

1 Cook pasta shells in boiling water in a large saucepan following package directions. Drain, set aside and keep warm.

2 To make sauce, heat oil in a large skillet and cook onions and garlic over a medium heat for 10 minutes or until onions are soft. Stir in wine and anchovies and bring to the boil. Boil for 2-3 minutes or until wine reduces by half.

3 Stir in rosemary and stock and bring back to the boil. Boil until sauces reduces and thickens slightly. Add chili and pasta to sauce, toss to combine, sprinkle with Parmesan cheese and serve immediately.

Serves 4

Anchovies come preserved in oil or salt. Once opened, canned anchovies can be kept, covered with olive oil, in the refrigerator. Anchovies preserved in salt should be rinsed well before using. In Italy and France fresh anchovies are popular.

Macaroni with Tomato Sauce

1 lb/500 g wholewheat macaroni

CHUNKY TOMATO SAUCE
2 tablespoons olive oil
1 onion, chopped
1 clove garlic, crushed
28 oz/810 g canned Italian-style tomatoes, undrained and mashed
1/4 cup/60 mL dry white wine
1 tablespoon chopped fresh basil
freshly ground black pepper

1 Cook macaroni in boiling water in a large saucepan following package directions. Drain, set aside and keep warm.

2 To make sauce, heat oil in a skillet and cook onion for 3-4 minutes or until soft. Stir in garlic, tomatoes and wine and cook, stirring constantly, over a medium heat for 5 minutes. Bring to the boil, then reduce heat and simmer, uncovered, for 10-15 minutes or until sauce reduces and thickens. Add basil and season to taste with black pepper.

3 Add sauce to hot macaroni and toss to combine. Serve immediately.

Serves 4

This fresh-tasting tomato sauce is delicious with any dried pasta. You might like to try serving it with bucatini, the Italian macaroni that is long like spaghetti, but thicker and hollow.

Red Pepper Frittata

Oven temperature
350°F, 180°C

7 oz/220 g fettuccine
1 1/2 cups/375 mL milk
1/2 cup/125 mL whipping cream
6 eggs, lightly beaten
2 tablespoons finely chopped fresh parsley
1 red pepper, chopped
freshly ground black pepper

1 Cook fettuccine in boiling water in a large saucepan following package directions. Drain and set aside.

2 Place milk, cream and eggs in a bowl and whisk to combine. Stir in parsley, red pepper, fettuccine and black pepper to taste.

3 Pour frittata mixture into a greased 9 in/23 cm shallow quiche or tart dish and bake for 25-30 minutes or until frittata is set.

Serves 4

Red Pepper Frittata

Rigatoni with Butternut Squash

Rigatoni with Butternut Squash

1 lb/500 g rigatoni
$^{1}/_{3}$ cup/90 g butter
8 oz/250 g butternut squash, cut into small cubes
1 tablespoon snipped fresh chives
pinch ground nutmeg
$^{1}/_{4}$ cup/30 g grated fresh Parmesan cheese
freshly ground black pepper

1 Cook rigatoni in boiling water in a large saucepan following package directions. Drain, set aside and keep warm.

2 Melt $^{1}/_{4}$ cup/60 g butter in a large saucepan and cook squash over a medium heat for 5-10 minutes or until tender.

3 Stir chives, nutmeg, Parmesan cheese, black pepper to taste, rigatoni and remaining butter into squash mixture and toss to combine. Serve immediately.

Serves 4

You might like to make this pasta dish using carrots or sweet potatoes instead of squash. The taste will be different, but just as delicious.

Spaghetti Carbonara

SPAGHETTI CARBONARA

6 oz/185 g sliced ham, cut into strips
4 eggs
1/3 cup/90 mL light cream (half and half)
3/4 cup/90 g grated fresh Parmesan cheese
1 lb/500 g spaghetti
freshly ground black pepper

1 Cook ham in a nonstick skillet for 2-3 minutes. Place eggs, cream and Parmesan cheese in a bowl and beat lightly to combine.

2 Cook spaghetti in boiling water in a large saucepan following package directions. Drain spaghetti, add egg mixture and ham and toss so that the heat of the spaghetti cooks the sauce. Season to taste with black pepper and serve immediately.

Serves 4

There are several stories concerning the origins of this classic dish. The most romantic of these is that it was a dish created by the 'carbonari' – or charcoal makers – of Italy. The story goes that, as the dish requires little cooking and all the ingredients are transportable, the carbonari were able to cook it over an open fire.

Macaroni with Basil

Macaroni with Basil

12 oz/375 g wholewheat macaroni
1 tablespoon olive oil
2 cloves garlic, crushed
8 oz/250 g button mushrooms, sliced
6 sun-dried tomatoes, drained and cut into strips
2 tablespoons chopped fresh basil
freshly ground black pepper

1 Cook macaroni in boiling water in a large saucepan following package directions. Drain, set aside and keep warm.

2 Heat oil in a large skillet and cook garlic, mushrooms and tomatoes over a medium heat for 4-5 minutes. Stir in basil and season to taste with black pepper.

3 Add macaroni to mushroom mixture and toss to combine. Serve immediately.

Serves 4

Basil originally came from India, where it is still regarded as a sacred herb. It was known in ancient times in southern Europe, and in Italy it symbolised love. Traditionally, a girl would place a pot in her window as an invitation to her lover to call on her.

TUNA-FILLED SHELLS

16 giant pasta shells

TUNA FILLING

8 oz/250 g ricotta cheese, drained
14 oz/440 g canned tuna in brine, drained and flaked
1/2 red pepper, diced
1 tablespoon chopped capers
1 teaspoon snipped fresh chives
4 tablespoons shredded Swiss cheese
pinch ground nutmeg
freshly ground black pepper
2 tablespoons grated fresh Parmesan cheese

1 Cook 8 pasta shells in a large saucepan of boiling water until al dente. Drain, rinse under cold running water and drain again. Set aside, not overlapping. Repeat with remaining shells.

2 To make filling, place ricotta cheese and tuna in a bowl and mix to combine. Mix in red pepper, capers, chives and 2 tablespoons shredded Swiss cheese, nutmeg and black pepper to taste.

3 Fill each shell with ricotta mixture, and place in a lightly greased, shallow ovenproof dish. Sprinkle with Parmesan cheese and remaining Swiss cheese. Place under a preheated broiler and cook until cheese melts.

Makes 16 filled shells

These filled shells are fun to eat hot or cold as finger food, or they can be served with a sauce as a first course.

Tuna-filled Shells

Spirelli with Ham

Spirelli with Ham

1 lb/500 g fresh or 13 oz/410 g dried spirelli or spiral pasta
2 teaspoons olive oil
10 oz/315 g ham, cut into strips
6 canned artichoke hearts, sliced lengthwise
3 eggs, beaten with 1 tablespoon grated fresh Parmesan cheese
freshly ground black pepper

1 Cook spirelli in boiling water in a large saucepan following package directions. Drain, set aside and keep warm.

2 Heat oil in a skillet and cook ham and artichokes for 1-2 minutes.

3 Add spirelli to pan and toss to combine. Remove from heat and quickly stir in egg mixture. Season to taste with black pepper. Serve as soon as the eggs start to stick to spirelli – this will take only a few seconds.

Serves 4

It is said that the four-pronged fork was invented by Ferdinand II, the King of Naples, so that spaghetti could be eaten in a more refined and elegant fashion.

Turkey Croquettes

3 oz/90 g butter
$1\frac{1}{3}$ cups/170 g all-purpose flour
1 cup/250 mL hot milk
4 oz/125 g ricotta cheese
8 oz/250 g cooked turkey, chopped
$\frac{1}{2}$ cup/60 g shredded mature Cheddar cheese
2 tablespoons chopped fresh parsley
1 cup/125 g dry bread crumbs
1 egg, lightly beaten
oil for deep-frying

Serves 4

1 Melt butter in a saucepan, stir in $\frac{1}{3}$ cup/45 g of the flour and cook, stirring, for 30 seconds. Whisk in milk and cook, stirring, over a medium heat for 4-5 minutes or until mixture thickens. Remove pan from heat and stir in ricotta cheese, turkey, Cheddar cheese and parsley. Mix well to combine and refrigerate until completely cold.

2 Place bread crumbs and remaining flour on separate plates and set aside. Shape turkey mixture into croquette shapes, roll each croquette in flour, then dip in egg and roll in bread crumbs. Place on a plate lined with plastic wrap, cover and chill for 15 minutes.

3 Heat oil in a large saucepan until hot and cook croquettes for 3-4 minutes or until golden.

Croquettes are a great way to use any leftover poultry or meat. In this recipe turkey has been used, but you could use leftover chicken, lamb or beef. Canned tuna or salmon are delicious alternatives. If using canned food, drain off any liquid first.

Turkey Croquettes

Summer Chicken Sauté

SUMMER CHICKEN SAUTE

2 tablespoons vegetable oil
1 onion, sliced
1 green pepper, cut into strips
1 red pepper, cut into strips
1 zucchini, sliced
$1^1/_2$ cups/375 mL tomato purée
1 tablespoon chopped fresh basil
1 tablespoon chopped fresh parsley
1 teaspoon chopped fresh thyme or $^1/_2$ teaspoon dried thyme
1 lb/500 g boned, skinned chicken breast halves, cut into strips
freshly ground black pepper

1 Heat oil in a large skillet and cook onion over a medium heat for 5 minutes or until soft. Add green and red pepper, zucchini and tomato purée and bring to the boil, then reduce heat and simmer for 10 minutes.

2 Stir in basil, parsley, thyme and chicken and cook for 10 minutes or until chicken is cooked. Season to taste with black pepper.

Serves 4

A medley of summer vegetables and chicken makes a quick and easy sauté that is delicious served with boiled noodles tossed in butter and finely chopped fresh parsley.

Chicken Stroganoff

CHICKEN STROGANOFF

1/3 cup/90 g butter
1 lb/500 g boneless skinned chicken breast halves, cut into strips
5 oz/155 g button mushrooms, halved
1/2 cup/125 mL dry white wine
1 cup/250 mL whipping cream
2 tablespoons tomato paste
1/2 teaspoon ground nutmeg
1 spring onion, finely chopped

1 Melt 1/4 cup/60 g butter in a large skillet and cook chicken, stirring, over a medium heat for 2-3 minutes or until chicken just changes color. Remove chicken from pan and set aside.

2 Melt remaining butter in pan and cook mushrooms for 2-3 minutes, then stir in wine, cream, tomato paste and nutmeg. Cook, stirring, over a high heat for 5 minutes or until sauce reduces and thickens slightly.

3 Add chicken to mushroom mixture and cook, stirring, over a medium heat, for 3-4 minutes or until chicken is cooked. Stir in spring onion and serve immediately.

Serves 4

Serve Chicken Stroganoff on a bed of boiled white or brown rice accompanied by a seasonal green vegetable – asparagus or green beans are delicious.

Chicken and Pimento Casserole

2 tablespoons vegetable oil
4 boned, skinned chicken breast halves, cut into strips
1 turnip, cut into strips
2 onions, chopped
14 oz/440 g canned pimentos, drained and cut into strips
1 cup/250 mL dry white wine
14 oz/440 g canned tomatoes, undrained and mashed
3 tablespoons chopped fresh basil

Serves 4

1 Heat oil in a large skillet and cook chicken, stirring, over a medium heat for 2-3 minutes or until chicken just changes color. Remove chicken from pan and set aside.

2 Add turnip, onions and pimentos to pan and cook for 3-4 minutes. Stir in wine and tomatoes and bring to the boil, stirring, over a medium heat, then reduce heat and simmer, uncovered, for 10 minutes or until turnip is tender. Return chicken to pan and cook for 3-4 minutes longer or until chicken is cooked. Stir in basil and serve immediately.

All this easy chicken dish needs to make a complete meal is hot garlic bread or crusty bread rolls and a salad of mixed lettuce and herbs.

Chicken and Pimento Casserole

Gnocchi with Herb Sauce

$1\frac{1}{2}$ lb/750 g gnocchi

FRESH HERB SAUCE
4 tablespoons chopped fresh parsley
4 tablespoons chopped fresh coriander
4 tablespoons chopped fresh basil
2 tablespoons pine nuts (pignola)
1 tablespoon grated Parmesan cheese
1 tablespoon mayonnaise
1 tablespoon chicken stock
freshly ground black pepper

Serves 4

1 Cook gnocchi in boiling water in a large saucepan following package directions. Drain, set aside and keep warm.

2 To make sauce, place parsley, coriander, basil, pine nuts (pignola) and Parmesan cheese in a food processor or blender and process to combine. Add mayonnaise and stock and process to combine. Season to taste with black pepper. Spoon sauce over gnocchi and serve immediately.

For a complete meal, accompany with a tossed green salad and wholewheat bread rolls.

Gnocchi with Herb Sauce

Cheesy Herb Soufflé

Cheesy Herb Souffle

3 tablespoons/45 g butter
1/4 cup/30 g all-purpose flour
1 cup/250 mL milk
1 1/4 cups/155 g shredded mature Cheddar cheese
2/3 cup/75 g grated Parmesan cheese
1/4 teaspoon ground nutmeg
4 tablespoons chopped fresh parsley
4 tablespoons snipped fresh chives
1 tablespoon finely chopped fresh basil
1 tablespoon chopped fresh coriander
freshly ground black pepper
4 eggs, separated

1 Melt butter in a large saucepan and cook flour over a medium heat for 1 minute. Gradually stir in milk and cook, stirring constantly, until sauce is thick and smooth.

2 Stir in mature Cheddar, Parmesan cheese, nutmeg, parsley, chives, basil, coriander and black pepper to taste, then beat in egg yolks one at a time.

3 Place egg whites in a clean bowl and beat until soft peaks form. Fold 2 tablespoons cheese mixture into egg whites, then fold egg white mixture into remaining cheese mixture.

4 Spoon soufflé mixture into a lightly greased 4 cup/1 liter capacity soufflé dish and bake for 25-30 minutes or until soufflé is puffed and golden. Serve immediately.

Serves 4

Oven temperature
400°F, 200°C

The secrets to successful soufflé-making are to make sure that the oven is at the correct temperature, the basic mixture is ready, and the soufflé dish is prepared before you beat the egg whites.

Coriander Beef Pitas

Of Middle Eastern origin, pita bread makes a wonderful container for any type of filling. The Coriander Hollandaise used in this recipe is also delicious served with baked fish, or you might prefer to make this recipe using fish in place of the beef. If using fish, use white wine in place of the red wine and steam, bake or microwave the fish until it flakes when tested with a fork.

1 lb/500 g sirloin steak, in one piece, trimmed of all visible fat
2 cloves garlic, crushed
1/3 cup/90 mL red wine
1/4 cup/60 mL olive oil
freshly ground black pepper
3 tablespoons chopped fresh coriander
4 large pita bread rounds, cut in half

CORIANDER HOLLANDAISE
2 cloves garlic
2 egg yolks
1 tablespoon lemon juice
2 tablespoons chopped fresh coriander
1 tablespoon chopped fresh parsley
1/2 cup/1 stick/125 g butter
freshly ground black pepper

1 Place steak in a shallow dish. Place garlic, wine, oil and black pepper to taste in a bowl and mix well to combine. Pour over steak, cover and set aside to marinate for 30 minutes. Drain steak and cook under a preheated broiler or on a preheated barbecue grill for 3-4 minutes each side or until cooked to your liking.

2 Slice steak diagonally across the grain and place in a bowl with coriander. Toss to combine. Fill pita breads with steak mixture.

3 To make hollandaise, place garlic, egg yolks, lemon juice, coriander and parsley in a food processor or blender and process to combine. Melt butter until hot and bubbling. With machine running, slowly pour in melted butter and process until thick. Season to taste with black pepper, then spoon over meat and serve immediately.

Serves 4

Coriander Beef Pitas

Leek and Dill Tart

10 oz/315 g prepared flaky pastry

LEEK FILLING
1 tablespoon/15 g butter
4 small leeks, trimmed and thinly sliced
1 cup/200 g plain yogurt
1 tablespoon flour
2 eggs, lightly beaten
3/4 cup/90 g shredded mature Cheddar cheese
3 tablespoons chopped fresh dill weed
freshly ground black pepper

1 Roll out pastry to line a lightly greased 8 in/20 cm loose-bottom tart pan. Prick base several times with a fork, line with nonstick parchment paper and fill with uncooked rice. Bake for 8-10 minutes, remove rice and paper and bake for 5 minutes longer or until pastry is golden. Set aside to cool.

2 To make filling, melt butter in a skillet and cook leeks for 4-5 minutes or until just tender.

3 Place yogurt, flour, eggs, three-quarters of the cheese and 1 tablespoon dill weed in a bowl and mix to combine. Fold in leeks, season to taste with black pepper and spoon into pastry case. Sprinkle with remaining cheese and dill weed and bake for 20 minutes or until tart is set.

Serves 4

Oven temperature
400°F, 200°C

Choose young thin leeks for this tart. The combination of young leeks and fresh dill weed gives the tart a garden-fresh taste.

Leek and Dill Tart

Pickled Vegetable Omelet

2 tablespoons peanut oil
8 oz/250 g lean ground beef
2 tablespoons bottled Chinese mixed vegetables (tung chai), drained and chopped
1 teaspoon honey
2 tablespoons soy sauce
6 spring onions, finely chopped
6 eggs, lightly beaten

1 Heat 1 tablespoon oil in a skillet and stir-fry beef, vegetables, honey, soy sauce and spring onions for 3-4 minutes or until cooked. Remove from pan, set aside and keep warm.

2 Heat remaining oil in a clean skillet, pour in one-quarter of the beaten eggs. Swirl pan over heat to make a thin omelet. Spoon one-quarter of the meat mixture into the center of the omelet and fold over the edges.

3 Remove omelet from pan, set aside and keep warm. Repeat with remaining eggs and meat mixture. Cut omelets into slices and serve immediately.

Serves 4

The Chinese mixed vegetables used as the filling for this omelet are available from most Oriental supermarkets.

Left: Eggplant Soufflé
Far left: Pickled Vegetable Omelet

Eggplant Souffle

5 tablespoons/75 g butter
2 cloves garlic, crushed
1 onion, finely chopped
1 large eggplant, peeled and finely chopped
1/2 cup/125 mL water
2 cups/500 mL milk
7 eggs
2 tablespoons all-purpose flour
1 cup/125 g shredded mature Cheddar cheese

Serves 4

1 Melt 3 tablespoons/45 g butter in a large skillet and cook garlic and onion for 2 minutes. Add eggplant and cook for 5 minutes longer. Add water to pan, cover and simmer over a low heat for 1 hour, stirring frequently, and adding more water if necessary.

2 Place 1 1/2 cups/375 mL milk and remaining butter in a saucepan and bring to the boil. Place remaining milk, 5 egg yolks, 2 whole eggs and flour in a bowl and whisk to combine. Slowly whisk egg mixture into boiling milk, reduce heat and cook, whisking constantly, until sauce thickens. Remove pan from heat and stir in eggplant mixture and cheese.

3 Place 5 egg whites in a bowl and beat until stiff peaks form. Fold egg whites into sauce, then spoon into a lightly greased 8 in/20 cm soufflé dish with collar attached. Bake for 35 minutes. Serve immediately.

Oven temperature
350°F, 180°C

The name 'eggplant' originated from the white variety of the fruit being about the same size, color and shape as an egg. Like tomatoes and sweet peppers, eggplant is a fruit that is treated as a vegetable.

Right: Baked Camembert
Below: Grilled Goat's Cheese Salad

Grilled Goat's Cheese Salad

1 radicchio, leaves separated
1 curly endive, leaves separated
14 oz/440 g canned artichoke hearts, drained and halved
8 cherry tomatoes, halved
2 oz/60 g button mushrooms
2 oz/60 g watercress, broken into sprigs
4 x $3^1/2$ oz/100 g goat's cheeses
1 tablespoon olive oil

HERB DRESSING
$1^1/2$ tablespoons lemon juice
$1^1/2$ tablespoons cider vinegar
$^1/2$ cup/125 mL olive oil
1 clove garlic, crushed
1 tablespoon chopped fresh basil or 1 teaspoon dried basil
2 teaspoons chopped fresh rosemary or $^1/2$ teaspoon dried rosemary
freshly ground black pepper

1 Arrange radicchio, endive, artichokes, tomatoes, mushrooms and watercress on individual serving plates.

2 To make dressing, place lemon juice, vinegar, oil, garlic, basil, rosemary and black pepper to taste in screwtop jar and shake well to combine.

3 Brush each goat's cheese with a little oil and cook under a preheated broiler for 1 minute each side or until cheese just starts to melt. Place cheese on top of salad, drizzle with dressing and serve.

Serves 4

Often known as chèvres, goat's cheeses can be eaten at different stages of ripening. A young cheese is soft and spreadable, maturing to being dry and somewhat crumbly; in fact it could be described as almost chalky.

Baked Camembert

8 oz/250 g wheel Camembert cheese
1 egg, lightly beaten
$^1/_4$ cup/30 g all-purpose flour, sifted
5 oz/155 g shelled pistachio nuts, chopped

RASPBERRY SAUCE
8 oz/250 g raspberries
1 tablespoon confectioners' sugar

1 To make sauce, place raspberries and confectioners' sugar in a food processor or blender and process until smooth. Push raspberry mixture through a sieve to remove seeds. Set aside until ready to serve.

2 Dip Camembert in egg, then roll in flour, dip in egg again and finally roll in pistachio nuts to coat. Place on a baking sheet lined with nonstick parchment paper and bake for 10-15 minutes or until cheese softens. Serve cut into wedges accompanied by raspberry sauce.

Serves 4 as a light meal, starter or dessert

Oven temperature
425°F, 220°C

This versatile dish can be served with a salad and crusty bread as a light meal, or on its own as a starter, or with additional berries for dessert. Whichever way you choose to serve it you can be assured that it will be popular. For something different, you might like to use slivered almonds in place of the pistachios.

Calamari in Tomato Sauce

1 tablespoon olive oil
1 lb/500 g calamari (squid) rings
1 onion, chopped
3 cloves garlic, crushed
4 tomatoes, peeled and chopped
2 teaspoons chopped fresh marjoram or $^{1}/_{2}$ teaspoon dried marjoram
1 bay leaf
1 cup/250 mL red wine
freshly ground black pepper

1 Heat oil in a large saucepan, add calamari (squid) and cook over a high heat for 3-4 minutes or until browned. Reduce heat to medium, add onion and garlic and cook, stirring, for 3-4 minutes longer or until onion is soft.

2 Add tomatoes, marjoram and bay leaf to calamari (squid) mixture and cook, stirring, for 5 minutes.

3 Stir in wine, cover and simmer for 1 hour or until calamari (squid) is tender. Season to taste with black pepper.

Serves 4

When buying fresh calamari (squid) it should have a good color, a slippery appearance and a fresh salty smell. Avoid calamari (squid) that has a broken outer skin or is lying in a pool of ink.

Tagliatelle with Tuna

12 oz/375 g dried wholewheat tagliatelle or spaghetti

TUNA SAUCE
1 onion, finely chopped
1 clove garlic, crushed
14 oz/440 g canned tomatoes, undrained and mashed
1 tablespoon tomato paste
1 tablespoon dry red wine
2 zucchini, sliced
14 oz/440 g canned water-packed tuna, drained and flaked
1 tablespoon finely shredded fresh basil
freshly ground black pepper

1 Cook pasta in boiling water in a large saucepan following package directions. Drain, set aside and keep warm.

2 To make sauce, heat a nonstick skillet and cook onion, garlic and 1 tablespoon of juice from tomatoes for 4-5 minutes or until onion is soft. Stir in tomatoes, tomato paste, wine and zucchini and cook over a low heat for 5 minutes.

3 Add tuna, basil and black pepper to taste to pan and cook for 5 minutes longer or until heated through. To serve, place pasta on serving plates and spoon sauce over.

Serves 4

When using canned water-packed tuna and salmon, drain off as much liquid as possible and add some cold water to the can. Drain off again and use fish as specified in the recipe. This removes over half the salt content and is handy when no-added-salt or salt-reduced products are unavailable.

Crumbed Fish Steaks, Tagliatelle with Tuna

Crumbed Fish Steaks

4 x 5 oz/155 g white fish steaks
2 tablespoons lime or lemon juice

HERB TOPPING
2 cups/125 g fresh wholewheat bread crumbs
$^1/_2$ cup/45 g instant rolled oats
2 tablespoons finely chopped fresh coriander
2 tablespoons snipped fresh chives
2 teaspoons olive oil
1 tablespoon vinegar
freshly ground black pepper

1 Brush steaks with lime or lemon juice and cook under a preheated broiler for 5 minutes on one side only.

2 To make topping, place bread crumbs, rolled oats, coriander, chives, oil, vinegar and black pepper to taste in a bowl and mix to combine.

3 Turn fish and top each steak with one-quarter of the topping. Broil for 5 minutes longer or until fish is cooked and topping is golden.

Serves 4

Serve garnished with slices or wedges of lemon and accompany with new potatoes and a green salad.

Paella

One of the traditional dishes of Spain, Paella varies from region to region and season to season. In Spain it is cooked in a large shallow paella dish; this ensures that the cooking liquid evaporates rapidly. A large skillet will do the same job.

1 tablespoon olive oil
2 cloves garlic, crushed
1 onion, chopped
3 tomatoes, chopped
1 red pepper, chopped
1 teaspoon paprika
1/4 teaspoon saffron powder or ground turmeric
5 oz/155 g long grain white rice
3 cups/750 mL chicken stock
8 oz/250 g cooked chicken, chopped
4 oz/125 g fresh or frozen peas
8 oz/250 g small shrimp, shelled
freshly ground black pepper

1 Heat oil in a large skillet, add garlic, onion, tomatoes and red pepper and cook over a medium heat for 5 minutes or until onion is soft.

2 Stir in paprika, saffron or turmeric and rice and cook for 3 minutes. Pour stock over rice mixture and bring to the boil. Reduce heat and simmer for 10 minutes or until rice is almost cooked.

3 Stir in chicken, peas and shrimp and cook for 5 minutes longer or until rice is tender and most of the liquid is absorbed. Serve immediately.

Serves 4

Left: Crispy Baked Fish
Below: Paella

Crispy Baked Fish

$1^1/_2$ lb/750 g firm white fish fillets, cut into $1^1/_4$ in/3 cm squares
freshly ground black pepper
3 tablespoons safflower or sunflower oil
2 cups/60 g corn flakes, crushed
1 tablespoon lemon juice

1 Using paper towels, pat fish dry. Place fish, black pepper to taste and oil in a bowl and toss to coat.

2 Roll each fish piece in crushed corn flakes and place in a single layer in a lightly oiled shallow baking dish.

3 Bake fish for 10-15 minutes or until cooked. Just prior to serving, sprinkle fish with lemon juice.

Serves 6

Oven temperature
400°F, 200°C

Using a fraction of the fat that is normally required to cook crumbed food, these fish pieces are sure to be popular with all those who are watching their fat intake. Whole fish fillets are also delicious prepared this way.

Lemon Spinach Fish Rolls

Oven temperature
350°F, 180°C

If evaporated skim milk is available, use it in this recipe to make a dish that is lower in calories (kilojoules).

1/4 cup/60 mL lemon juice
2 cloves garlic, crushed
freshly ground black pepper
8 x 2-2 1/2 oz/60-75 g thin white fish fillets
16 large spinach leaves, stems removed
1 tablespoon snipped fresh chives

LEMON SAUCE
2 tablespoons lemon juice
1/2 cup/125 mL evaporated milk
2 teaspoons cornstarch

1 Place lemon juice, garlic and black pepper to taste in a small bowl and whisk to combine. Brush each fillet with lemon juice mixture, then top with 2 spinach leaves, folding them to fit the fillets.

2 Roll up fillets and secure with wooden toothpicks. Place rolls in a lightly oiled, shallow baking dish and bake for 20 minutes or until fish is cooked. Remove fish from dish, set aside and keep warm. Reserve cooking juices.

3 To make sauce, place the reserved cooking juices, lemon juice, evaporated milk, cornstarch and black pepper to taste in a small saucepan and cook over a medium heat, stirring constantly, for 3-4 minutes or until sauce boils and thickens slightly. Spoon sauce over rolls, sprinkle with chives and serve immediately.

Serves 4

Left: Smoked Salmon Risotto
Below: Lemon Spinach Fish Rolls

Smoked Salmon Risotto

1 tablespoon olive oil
2 onions, chopped
2 cloves garlic, crushed
$^{1}/_{4}$ teaspoon ground turmeric
1 $^{1}/_{2}$ cups/330 g short grain rice
1 red pepper, chopped
3 cups/750 mL fish or chicken stock
3 spring onions, chopped
1 tablespoon chopped fresh basil
1 tablespoon snipped fresh chives
8 slices smoked salmon, cut into strips
freshly ground black pepper

1 Heat oil in a large nonstick skillet, add onions, garlic and turmeric, and stir over a medium heat for 4-5 minutes or until onions start to soften.

2 Add rice and red pepper and cook, stirring, for 3 minutes longer. Add stock, bring to simmering and simmer, uncovered, for 20 minutes or until rice is tender.

3 Stir in spring onions, basil, chives, salmon and black pepper to taste. Serve immediately.

Serves 4

A risotto is a great one-dish meal. Accompanied by a tossed salad of mixed lettuces and herbs and a glass of dry white wine, this risotto is a delicious summer lunch dish.

Curried Chicken Kabobs

For a complete meal serve kabobs, a mixed lettuce salad and garlic baked potatoes.
To make potatoes, scrub the required number of large potatoes and, using an apple corer, carefully remove a plug from each potato, making sure not to go right through the potato. Reserve the plugs. For each potato you will require 1 clove garlic, halved. Combine 2 tablespoons olive oil, 1 tablespoon finely chopped fresh rosemary and freshly ground black pepper to taste. Fill hole in each potato with two garlic halves and a little oil mixture. Cut off two-thirds of the plug and discard. Replace remaining plug in potato and wrap potatoes in aluminum foil. Cook potatoes on a preheated barbecue grill or in the oven at 350°F/180°C for 1 hour or until tender.

1 1/2 lb/750 g boned, skinned chicken breast halves, skin removed, cut into 1 in/2.5 cm cubes

LIME CURRY GLAZE
1 cup/315 g lime marmalade
2 tablespoons Dijon mustard
2 teaspoons curry powder
1 tablespoon lime juice

1 To make glaze, place marmalade, mustard, curry powder and lime juice in a small saucepan and cook over a medium heat, stirring, for 3 minutes or until ingredients are combined. Remove from heat and set aside to cool.

2 Thread chicken cubes onto twelve oiled skewers. Place skewers in a shallow glass or ceramic dish, spoon glaze over, cover and set aside to marinate for at least an hour.

3 Remove chicken from glaze and reserve any remaining glaze. Cook kabobs on a lightly oiled, preheated barbecue, turning frequently and brushing with reserved marinade for 8-10 minutes or until cooked.

Makes 12

Seafood Kabobs

Kabobs can be cooked under a preheated broiler rather than on the barbecue if you wish.

8 mussels, removed from shells
1 large white fish fillet, cut into 8 x 3/4 in/2 cm cubes
8 large uncooked shrimp, shelled and deveined, tails left intact
8 scallops
1 salmon fillet, cut into 8 x 3/4 in/2 cm cubes

CHILI LIME GLAZE
1/4 cup/60 mL olive oil
2 fresh red chilies, seeded and finely chopped
1 clove garlic, crushed
1/4 cup/60 mL lime juice

1 Thread a mussel, a piece of white fish, a shrimp, a scallop and a piece of salmon on to an oiled skewer. Repeat with remaining seafood to make eight skewers.

2 To make glaze, place oil, chilies, garlic and lime juice in a small bowl and mix to combine.

3 Brush kabobs with glaze and cook on a lightly oiled, preheated barbecue grill, turning frequently and brushing with remaining glaze, for 4-5 minutes or until seafood changes color and is cooked through. Serve immediately.

Makes 8

Seafood Kabobs,
Curried Chicken Kabobs

French Omelet

For best results, prepare and cook omelets quickly and serve immediately. Remember, if the heat is too high, or the omelet is cooked for too long, it will be tough and dry. Try one of these delicious fillings or make your own favorite combinations.

2 eggs
1 tablespoon cold water
freshly ground black pepper
1 tablespoon/15 g butter

1 Place eggs, water and black pepper to taste in a bowl and whisk lightly to combine.

2 Heat an omelet pan over a medium heat until hot. Add butter, tipping the pan so the base is completely coated. Heat until the butter is foaming, but not browned, then add the egg mixture. As it sets use a palette knife or fork to gently draw up the edge of the omelet until no liquid remains and the omelet is lightly set.

3 Serve omelet plain, or topped with filling of your choice, and fold in half. Slip omelet onto a plate and serve immediately.

Serves 1

Avocado and Bacon Filling

1 tablespoon dairy sour cream or plain yogurt
1 teaspoon snipped fresh chives
1/2 teaspoon Dijon mustard
1 slice bacon, chopped
1/4 avocado, stoned, peeled and chopped

1 Place sour cream or yogurt, chives and mustard in a bowl and mix to combine. Cook bacon in a small skillet for 2-3 minutes or until crisp. Remove and drain on paper towels.

2 Spread sour cream or yogurt mixture over one half of an omelet and top with bacon and avocado. Fold omelet and serve immediately.

Vegetarian Filling

The simplest of all fillings for an omelet is freshly chopped herbs, either a single herb or a mixture. Herbs that are delicious with eggs include basil, parsley, chives, dill weed, mint, thyme and marjoram.

1 teaspoon olive oil
1 tablespoon chopped green pepper
1 tablespoon finely chopped onion
1 small clove garlic, crushed
1/2 tomato, peeled and chopped
1 black olive, sliced
1 teaspoon finely chopped fresh basil
freshly ground black pepper

1 Heat oil in a small skillet and cook green pepper, onion and garlic over a medium heat for 2-3 minutes or until onion is soft. Add tomato, olive and basil and cook for 5 minutes longer. Season to taste with black pepper.

2 Place filling on one half of an omelet, fold and serve immediately.

French Omelet with Avocado and Bacon Filling, and Vegetarian Filling

RECIPE COLLECTION

Vegetarian

Rice, beans and grains should form the basis of a balanced vegetarian diet. Eggs and cheese are also important foods for many vegetarians. You will find the recipes in this section rely on these foods to make delicious and nutritious dishes.

Lentil Salad, Red Hot Beans

Lentil Salad

1 cup/185 g red lentils
1 cup/185 g yellow lentils
6 cups/1.5 liters vegetable stock
1 teaspoon cumin seeds
2 tomatoes, diced
2 stalks celery, sliced
1/2 green pepper, diced
1/2 red pepper, diced
1 small onion, chopped
1 small avocado, stoned, peeled and chopped
2 tablespoons snipped fresh chives

SPICY DRESSING
1/4 teaspoon ground coriander
1/4 teaspoon ground turmeric
pinch chili powder
1 clove garlic, crushed
4 tablespoons cider vinegar
1 tablespoon olive oil
freshly ground black pepper

1 Place red and yellow lentils, stock and cumin seeds in a saucepan and bring to the boil. Reduce heat and simmer for 20 minutes or until lentils are tender. Drain and set aside to cool.

2 Place cold lentils, tomatoes, celery, green and red pepper, onion and avocado in a large salad bowl.

3 To make dressing, place coriander, turmeric, chili powder, garlic, vinegar, oil and black pepper to taste in a screwtop jar and shake well to combine. Spoon dressing over salad and toss to combine. Sprinkle with chives and serve immediately.

Serves 6

Dried peas, beans and lentils are often avoided because they cause embarrassing flatulence (wind). This can be considerably reduced by discarding soaking water, rinsing beans, and adding fresh water for cooking. The flatulence is caused by certain food components in legumes, which are not fully digested, and end up being broken down into gases in the bowel.

Red Hot Beans

1 1/4 cups/250 g dried red kidney beans
1 eggplant, diced
1 red pepper, cut into strips
1 onion, sliced
1 clove garlic, crushed
4 large tomatoes, skinned and chopped
2 tablespoons tomato paste
2 teaspoons chili sauce
1 cup/250 mL water
freshly ground black pepper
2 tablespoons chopped fresh coriander

1 Place beans in a large bowl, cover with water and set aside to soak overnight, then drain.

2 Place beans, eggplant, red pepper, onion, garlic, tomatoes, tomato paste, chili sauce and water in a large saucepan and bring to the boil. Boil for 15 minutes then reduce heat and simmer, stirring occasionally, for 1 hour or until beans are tender. Season to taste with black pepper and sprinkle with coriander.

Serves 4

The hotness of Red Hot Beans can be altered according to taste. If you are unsure, carefully add chili sauce a little at a time, tasting until it is right. Serve with bowls of plain yogurt.

Risotto Primavera

12 oz/375 g yellow baby squash, cut into quarters or 2 carrots, sliced
4 zucchini, sliced
8 oz/250 g asparagus spears, cut into 1 in/2.5 cm pieces
2 red peppers, cut into quarters
freshly ground black pepper
3 tablespoons grated Parmesan cheese

RISOTTO

1/2 cup/1 stick/125 g butter
2 leeks, sliced
2 cloves garlic, crushed
2 1/2 cups/500 g Arborio or risotto rice
1 cup/250 mL dry white wine
1/4 cup/60 mL tarragon vinegar
2 bay leaves
3 cups/750 mL chicken or vegetable stock
6 sun-dried tomatoes, chopped or 2 tomatoes, peeled and chopped
1 tablespoon chopped fresh basil

1 To make Risotto, melt butter in a heavy-based saucepan, add leeks and garlic and cook over a medium heat for 5 minutes or until leeks are soft. Stir in rice, tossing well to coat with butter.

2 Stir in wine and vinegar, bring to simmering and simmer until most of the liquid is absorbed. Add bay leaves and 2 cups/500 mL stock. Simmer until liquid is absorbed. Stir in tomatoes and remaining stock and simmer, stirring frequently, until liquid is absorbed and rice is tender. Stir in basil and black pepper to taste.

3 Boil, steam or microwave squash, zucchini and asparagus separately until tender. Set aside and keep warm. Broil red peppers, skin side up until skin blisters. Peel and slice thickly. Toss vegetables together and season to taste with black pepper. To serve, place Risotto on a serving plate and surround with vegetables. Sprinkle with Parmesan cheese.

Serves 8

Arborio rice is an Italian short grain rice from the Po Valley. Short grain rice contains more starch than long and medium grain rice and so becomes sticky as it cooks. Arborio absorbs liquid without becoming soft and it is this special quality that makes it most suitable for risottos. Arborio rice is recognisable by the distinctive white spot on each kernel. If it is unavailable, short grain rice can be used instead.

'A wedge of fresh Parmesan served with ripe pears makes a wonderful finish to any meal.'

Risotto Primavera, Cheese and Onion Strata

Cheese and Onion Strata

VEGETARIAN

2 tablespoons/30 g butter
3 large onions, thinly sliced
1/2 teaspoon dried thyme
1/2 cup/60 g grated Parmesan cheese
1/2 cup/60 g shredded smoked cheese
1 cup/125 g shredded mature Cheddar cheese
1 tablespoon snipped fresh chives
8 slices wholewheat bread, crusts removed
3 eggs
2 cups/500 mL milk
freshly ground black pepper

Serves 6

1 Melt butter in a skillet, add onions and thyme and cook over a low heat, stirring frequently, for 10-15 minutes or until onions are golden and soft.

2 Place Parmesan, smoked and Cheddar cheeses and chives in a bowl and toss to combine. Place half the bread in the base of a greased baking dish, cutting slices to fit snugly, if necessary. Cover with onion mixture and sprinkle with half the cheese mixture. Repeat with remaining bread and cheese.

3 Place eggs and milk in a bowl and whisk to combine. Season to taste with black pepper. Pour egg mixture over bread and cheese in baking dish and bake for 30-35 minutes or until firm and golden.

Oven temperature
375°F, 190°C

This delicious savory version of bread pudding is a great way to use up day-old bread and to make the most of any oddments of cheese. You might like to try other cheeses, such as blue, Camembert or Gouda, depending upon what you have in your refrigerator.

Cheese Roulade

Oven temperature
400°F, 200°C

2 zucchini, shredded
4 eggs, separated
2 tablespoons shredded Gruyère cheese
3 tablespoons grated Parmesan cheese
1/2 teaspoon ground nutmeg
freshly ground black pepper

CHEESE FILLING
2 tablespoons/30 g butter
1/4 cup/30 g all-purpose flour
1 1/4 cups/315 mL milk
6 oz/185 g ricotta or full-fat soft cheese, drained

1 To make filling, melt butter in a saucepan over a medium heat and cook flour for 1 minute. Remove pan from heat and stir in milk. Return pan to a low heat and cook, stirring, for 4-5 minutes or until sauce boils and thickens. Remove 2 tablespoons of sauce and set aside to use for the roulade. Stir ricotta or full-fat soft cheese into remaining sauce and set aside.

2 Cook zucchini in 2 tablespoons of water or in the microwave until soft. Drain and pat dry using paper towels. Place zucchini, reserved 2 tablespoons sauce, egg yolks, Gruyère cheese, Parmesan cheese, nutmeg and black pepper to taste in a bowl and mix to combine.

3 Place egg whites in a clean bowl and beat until stiff peaks form. Fold egg white mixture into zucchini mixture. Spoon into a greased and lined 10 x 12 in/ 25 x 30 cm jelly roll pan and bake for 12-15 minutes or until roulade is set. Turn roulade onto a wire rack covered with a clean teatowel and, while still warm, roll up from short end, jelly roll style. Hold for 30 seconds then unroll. Carefully remove paper and teatowel and set roulade aside to cool for 5 minutes. Spread filling evenly over roulade and roll up again. Serve at room temperature.

Serves 6

An elegant luncheon dish, this roulade makes entertaining easy and is sure to impress. It can be made several hours ahead of time and is delicious served with a julienne of vegetables.

'One of the easiest ways to separate eggs is to give the shell a sharp tap with a knife and then to allow the white to drain slowly through the hole.'

Corn and Chili Soufflé

CORN AND CHILI SOUFFLE

3 tablespoons fresh bread crumbs
1/4 cup/1/2 stick/60 g butter
1 onion, finely chopped
1 red chili, seeds removed and finely chopped
1/4 cup/30 g all-purpose flour
1/2 cup/125 mL/4 fl oz milk
10 oz/315 g canned creamed sweet corn
4 egg yolks
freshly ground black pepper
5 egg whites

Serves 4

1 Grease a 7 in/18 cm soufflé dish, sprinkle with bread crumbs and set aside.

2 Melt butter in a saucepan and cook onion and chili over a medium heat for 10 minutes, or until onion is soft and golden. Stir in flour and cook for 1 minute longer. Remove pan from heat and gradually stir in milk and corn. Return to heat and cook, stirring constantly, until mixture boils and thickens. Remove from heat and beat in egg yolks one at a time. Season to taste with black pepper.

3 Place egg whites in a bowl and beat until stiff peaks form. Fold gently into corn mixture.

4 Spoon soufflé mixture into prepared dish and bake for 30-35 minutes or until soufflé is puffed and golden. Serve immediately.

Oven temperature
400°F, 200°C

To test if a soufflé is cooked, shake the dish gently. If the soufflé wobbles all over, cook for 5 minutes longer. Always serve a soufflé immediately it is cooked.

Vegetable Tart

Oven temperature
350°F, 180°C

6 oz/185 g prepared wholewheat short (flaky) pastry
2 tablespoons/30 g butter
1 tablespoon flour
1¼ cups/315 mL milk
10 oz/315 g canned sweet corn kernels, drained
4 oz/125 g fresh or frozen peas, cooked
4 spring onions, chopped
freshly ground black pepper
2 eggs
1 cup/125 g shredded mature Cheddar cheese

1 Roll out pastry to fit a 9 in/23 cm tart pan with removable base. Prick pastry shell with a fork, line with nonstick parchment paper and fill with uncooked rice. Bake for 8 minutes, then remove rice and paper and bake for 10 minutes longer or until pastry is golden.

2 Melt butter in a saucepan and cook flour for 1 minute. Gradually stir in milk and cook over a medium heat, stirring constantly, for 4-5 minutes or until mixture boils and thickens. Add corn, peas, spring onions and black pepper to taste, then mix in eggs.

3 Pour corn mixture into pastry shell, sprinkle with cheese and bake for 30 minutes or until set and golden.

Serves 4

Did you know? The color of an eggshell depends on the breed of the hen and has no bearing on the nutritional value of the egg.

Far left: Vegetable Tart
Left: Cheese and Chives Soufflé

Cheese and Chives Souffles

1/4 cup/1/2 stick/60 g butter
1/2 cup/60 g all-purpose flour
1 1/4 cups/315 mL hot milk
1 cup/125 g shredded mature Cheddar cheese
1 teaspoon ground nutmeg
3 eggs, separated
2 tablespoons snipped fresh chives

1 Melt butter in a saucepan and cook flour over a medium heat, stirring constantly for 1 minute. Reduce heat, stir in hot milk and whisk over a low heat until sauce is smooth and thickens.

2 Remove pan from heat and set aside to cool for 10 minutes. Stir in cheese, nutmeg, egg yolks and chives.

3 Place egg whites in a bowl and beat until soft peaks form. Fold egg white mixture into sauce. Divide soufflé mixture between six greased and collared 1/2 cup/185 mL capacity soufflé dishes and bake for 15-20 minutes or until soufflés are puffed and golden.

Serves 6

Oven temperature
400°F, 200°C

For the best volume have egg whites at room temperature before beating. Egg whites for a soufflé should be beaten until they are stiff but not dry.

Spinach Roulade

Oven temperature
400°F, 200°C

Eggs have always been a symbol of new life and prosperity. It is said that if you dream about eggs then the future will bring riches and good luck. However, beware if the eggs you dream about are broken or cracked, as this indicates you will quarrel with your lover.

8 oz/250 g frozen spinach, thawed
1 tablespoon all-purpose flour
5 eggs, separated
1 tablespoon/15 g butter
1 teaspoon ground nutmeg
freshly ground black pepper
2 tablespoons grated Parmesan cheese

MUSHROOM FILLING
2 tablespoons/30 g butter
4 oz/125 g button mushrooms, sliced
3 spring onions, chopped
14 oz/440 g canned tomatoes, drained and mashed
1 teaspoon chopped fresh oregano or 1/2 teaspoon dried oregano
2 teaspoons chopped fresh basil or 1/2 teaspoon dried basil
freshly ground black pepper

1 Place spinach, flour, egg yolks, butter, nutmeg and black pepper to taste in a food processor or blender and process until combined. Transfer to a bowl.

2 Place egg whites in a bowl and beat until stiff peaks form, then mix 2 tablespoons of egg whites into spinach mixture. Fold remaining egg whites into spinach mixture. Spoon into a greased and lined 10 x 12 in/25 x 30 cm jelly roll pan and cook for 12 minutes or until firm.

3 To make filling, melt butter in a skillet and cook mushrooms over a medium heat for 1 minute. Add spring onions, tomatoes, oregano, basil and black pepper to taste, and cook for 3 minutes longer.

4 Turn roulade onto a teatowel, sprinkle with Parmesan cheese and roll up. Allow to stand for 1 minute. Unroll and spread with filling. Reroll and serve immediately.

Serves 6

Below: Vegetable Bake
Bottom left: Spinach Roulade

Vegetable Bake

2 zucchini, shredded
1 large potato, grated
1 green pepper, finely chopped
2 stalks celery, finely chopped
1 leek, thinly sliced
2 slices multiwheat bread, crumbed
1/2 cup/60 g shredded mature Cheddar cheese
3 eggs, lightly beaten
3 tablespoons chopped fresh dill weed
freshly ground black pepper

1 Place zucchini, potato, green pepper, celery, leek, bread crumbs, cheese, eggs and dill weed in a large bowl and mix to combine. Season to taste with black pepper.

2 Spoon mixture into a lightly greased baking dish and bake for 45-50 minutes or until firm.

Serves 4

Oven temperature
400°F, 200°C

This Vegetable Bake is delicious eaten hot, warm or cold. Cold, it makes a wonderful picnic dish and is delicious accompanied by a tomato salad.

Vegetable and Egg Stir-Fry

Often called Egg Foo Yung and traditionally made with shrimp, fish or beef, this popular recipe is delicious just made with vegetables.

4 oz/125 g snow peas, trimmed
6 oz/185 g asparagus spears, cut into 2 in/5 cm pieces
3 eggs
1 teaspoon sesame oil
1/4 cup/60 mL water
1 teaspoon dry sherry
1 teaspoon soy sauce
freshly ground black pepper
1 tablespoon vegetable oil
3 spring onions, chopped

1 Boil, steam or microwave snow peas and asparagus separately until just tender. Drain and refresh under cold running water. Drain again and set aside.

2 Place eggs, sesame oil, water, sherry, soy sauce and black pepper to taste in a bowl and whisk lightly to combine.

3 Heat vegetable oil in a wok or skillet, add egg mixture and stir-fry for 1 minute or until egg mixture just begins to set. Add snow peas, asparagus and spring onions and stir-fry for 1 minute longer. Serve immediately.

Serves 2

Blue Cheese Omelet

Cheese and apples are natural partners; as a filling in this omelet, they are an extra-special combination.

1 tablespoon/15 g butter
2 eggs
2 teaspoons water
freshly ground black pepper

CHEESE AND APPLE FILLING
1 tablespoon/15 g butter
1/2 small green apple, cored and thinly sliced
1/4 cup/30 g crumbled blue cheese
1 teaspoon snipped fresh chives

1 To make filling, melt butter in a small skillet and cook apple over a low heat for 2-3 minutes or until just heated through. Remove pan from heat, set aside and keep warm.

2 To make omelet, melt butter in a small skillet. Place eggs, water and black pepper to taste in a small bowl and whisk to combine. Pour egg mixture into pan and cook over a medium heat, continually drawing in the edge of the omelet with a fork during cooking, until no liquid remains and the omelet is lightly set.

3 Top half the omelet with apple slices, cheese and chives and fold in half. Slip onto a plate and serve immediately.

Serves 1

Indian Egg Curry

VEGETARIAN

6 hard-cooked eggs, halved lengthwise

CURRY SAUCE
1 tablespoon vegetable oil
1 large onion, finely chopped
1 clove garlic, crushed
1 tablespoon finely chopped fresh ginger
1 teaspoon ground cumin
1 teaspoon ground coriander
1/2 teaspoon chili powder
1 teaspoon ground turmeric
14 oz/440 g canned tomatoes, undrained and mashed
1/2 cup/125 mL coconut milk
freshly ground black pepper

1 To make sauce, heat oil in a skillet and cook onion, garlic and ginger over a medium heat for 5 minutes or until onion softens. Stir in cumin, coriander, chili powder and turmeric, and cook for 2 minutes longer.

2 Add tomatoes and coconut milk, bring to the boil, then reduce heat and simmer for 15 minutes or until sauce reduces and thickens. Season to taste with black pepper.

3 Place eggs in a shallow baking dish and spoon sauce over. Cover and bake for 20 minutes or until heated through.

Serves 6

Oven temperature
350°F, 180°C

A delicious egg curry that combines all the tastes of India. For a complete meal, accompany with steamed or boiled white or brown rice.

Indian Egg Curry, Vegetable and Egg Stir-Fry

Rice Fritters

Serve these fritters with hummus or a dipping sauce made of plain yogurt and flavored with chopped fresh mint and freshly ground black pepper.
Besan flour is made from chickpeas (garbanzo beans) and can be found in Asian specialty food stores and health food shops. All-purpose flour could be used in place of the besan flour if you wish.

1/4 teaspoon chili powder
1 teaspoon garam masala
1/2 cup/75 g wholewheat flour
2/3 cup/75 g besan flour
1/2 cup/100 g brown rice, cooked
2 eggs, lightly beaten
3/4 cup/185 mL milk
4 spring onions, chopped
1/2 small red pepper, chopped
freshly ground black pepper
vegetable oil for shallow-frying

1 Sift chili powder, garam masala and wholewheat and besan flours together into a bowl. Mix in rice, then make a well in the center and gradually stir in eggs and milk. Mix to make a smooth batter, then stir in spring onions, red pepper and black pepper to taste.

2 Heat oil in a large skillet and cook spoonfuls of batter for 3-4 minutes each side or until golden. Drain on paper towels and serve immediately.

Makes 20

Mung Bean Frittata

If commercially made coconut milk is unavailable, you can make it using grated fresh or dry coconut and water. To make coconut milk, place 1 lb/500 g coconut in a bowl and pour over 3 cups/750 mL boiling water. Leave to stand for 30 minutes, then strain, squeezing the coconut to extract as much liquid as possible. This will make a thick coconut milk. The coconut can be used again to make a weaker coconut milk.

3 1/2 oz/100 g dried mung beans
2 eggs
2 tablespoons vegetable oil
1 onion, sliced
2 potatoes, shredded
2 carrots, shredded
2 zucchini, shredded
4 oz/125 g canned sweet corn kernels, drained
3 tablespoons chopped fresh basil
freshly ground black pepper
1 cup/125 g shredded mature Cheddar chesse

COCONUT CREAM
1/2 cup/125 mL coconut milk
1 tablespoon lemon juice
2 tablespoons chopped fresh mint

1 Place mung beans in a bowl, pour over boiling water to cover and set aside to soak for 30 minutes. Drain beans and place in a food processor or blender with eggs and process until smooth. Transfer to a large bowl.

2 Heat 1 tablespoon oil in a skillet, add onion and cook over a low heat for 3-4 minutes. Add potatoes, carrots and zucchini and cook, stirring, for 5 minutes or until vegetables are tender. Remove vegetables from pan and drain on paper towels.

3 Add cooked vegetables, sweet corn, basil and black pepper to taste to bean mixture and mix well to combine.

4 Heat remaining oil in a large nonstick skillet, add vegetable mixture, sprinkle with cheese and cook over a low heat for 5-8 minutes or until just firm. Place pan under a preheated broiler and cook for 3 minutes or until top of frittata is browned.

5 To make Coconut Cream, place coconut milk, lemon juice and mint in a screwtop jar and shake well to combine. Invert frittata onto a serving plate, cut into wedges and serve with Coconut Cream.

Serves 6

Mung Bean Frittata,
Rice Fritters

Spicy Vegetable Loaf

Oven temperature
350°F, 180°C

Legumes supply valuable amounts of B group vitamins, especially vitamin B, B6, niacin and folic acid. Their iron content is fairly high, but occurs in an inorganic form, not well absorbed by the human body. Eating a food high in vitamin C (such as orange juice or a salad) at the same meal as legumes increases the absorption of iron.

1 tablespoon olive oil
1 clove garlic, crushed
1 onion, chopped
1/2 teaspoon chili powder
1/2 teaspoon ground cumin
1/2 teaspoon ground coriander
1/2 teaspoon ground turmeric
2 1/2 cups/500 g red lentils
1 carrot, shredded
1 large potato, shredded
14 oz/440 g canned tomatoes, undrained and mashed
2 cups/500 mL vegetable stock
3 egg whites
1 1/2 cups/140 g rolled oats
freshly ground black pepper

1 Heat oil in a large skillet, add garlic, onion, chili powder, cumin, coriander and turmeric and cook for 4-5 minutes or until onion is soft.

2 Add lentils, carrot, potato, tomatoes and stock and bring to the boil. Reduce heat, cover and simmer for 30 minutes or until lentils are tender. Remove pan from heat and set aside to cool slightly.

3 Place egg whites in a bowl and beat until stiff peaks form. Fold egg whites into lentil mixture.

4 Stir rolled oats into lentil mixture and season to taste with black pepper. Spoon into a lightly greased 4 1/2 x 8 1/2 in/11 x 21 cm in loaf pan and bake for 1 hour.

Serves 6

Vegetable and Lentil Curry

When cooking beans and rice, cook extra as these can be frozen and added to dishes as required.

1 tablespoon olive oil
1 onion, sliced
1 clove garlic, crushed
1 teaspoon ground cumin
1 teaspoon ground coriander
1 teaspoon ground turmeric
2 carrots, sliced
1/2 cup/100 g red lentils
14 oz/440 g canned tomatoes, undrained and mashed
1 1/2 cups/375 mL vegetable stock or water
1 teaspoon chili sauce, or according to taste
1 lb/500 g butternut squash or sweet potatoes, cut into 3/4 in/2 cm cubes
1/2 small cauliflower, cut into florets
2 tablespoons blanched almonds
freshly ground black pepper
4 tablespoons plain yogurt

1 Heat oil in a large saucepan, add onion, garlic, cumin, coriander, turmeric and carrots and cook for 5 minutes or until onion is soft.

2 Stir in lentils, tomatoes and stock or water and bring to the boil. Reduce heat, cover and simmer for 15 minutes.

3 Add chili sauce, squash or sweet potatoes and cauliflower and cook for 15-20 minutes longer or until squash is tender. Stir in almonds and black pepper to taste. To serve, ladle curry into bowls and top with a spoonful of yogurt.

Serves 4

Spicy Vegetable Loaf,
Vegetable and Lentil Curry

Right: Potato-filled Peppers
Far right: Vegetarian Chili

Potato-filled Peppers

Oven temperature
350°F, 180°C

6 green or red peppers
1/4 cup/1/2 stick/60 g butter
1 small fresh red chili, seeded and chopped
1 onion, chopped
4 potatoes, cooked, peeled and cubed
1/2 teaspoon ground coriander
1/4 teaspoon ground cumin
1/2 teaspoon mustard seeds
1/2 teaspoon ground turmeric
1/2 teaspoon garam masala
2 teaspoons lemon juice

1 Cut a slice from the top of each pepper. Remove seeds, keeping shells intact. Drop peppers into a saucepan of boiling water and cook for 3 minutes. Drain, refresh under cold running water and pat dry with paper towels.

2 Melt butter in a large skillet, add chili, onion and potatoes and stir-fry over a medium heat for 5 minutes or until potatoes are golden brown. Stir in coriander, cumin, mustard seeds, turmeric and garam masala and cook, stirring, for 1-2 minutes longer. Sprinkle with lemon juice.

3 Spoon potato mixture into pepper shells, place shells in a lightly greased baking dish and bake for 20 minutes.

Serves 6

The secret to this recipe is the garam masala. Garam masala is a highly scented mix of cardamom seeds, cinnamon stick, nutmeg, mace and cumin seeds. Sometimes cloves and coriander are added for extra zest. It can be found in the herb and spice section of any supermarket.

Vegetarian Chili

2 tablespoons vegetable oil
2 onions, cut into eighths
3 cloves garlic, crushed
2 carrots, sliced
1 red pepper, chopped
1 green pepper, chopped
8 oz/250 g butternut squash, diced
2 teaspoons chili paste (sambal oelek)
1 teaspoon dried oregano
2 teaspoons ground cumin
4 tomatoes, cut into eighths
3 tablespoons tomato paste
1/2 cup/125 mL tomato catsup
2 tablespoons Worcestershire sauce
2 cups/500 mL vegetable stock or water
28 oz/810 g canned red kidney beans, drained and rinsed
8 oz/250 g green beans, cut into 1 in/2.5 cm lengths
8 oz/250 g baby squash, quartered
4 zucchini, sliced
freshly ground black pepper
2 avocados, halved, pitted and peeled
1 tablespoon lemon juice
1 cup/250 g dairy sour cream or plain yogurt

1 Heat oil in a large saucepan, add onions and garlic and cook for 5 minutes or until onions are soft. Add carrots, red and green pepper and butternut squash and cook for 5 minutes longer.

2 Stir in chili paste (sambal oelek), oregano, cumin, tomatoes, tomato paste, tomato catsup, Worcestershire sauce, stock or water and red kidney beans and bring to the boil. Reduce heat, cover and simmer for 25 minutes or until vegetables are almost tender. Add green beans, baby squash and zucchini and cook for 10 minutes longer or until all vegetables are tender. Season to taste with black pepper.

3 Place avocados, lemon juice and black pepper to taste in a bowl and mash. Serve avocado mixture and sour cream or yogurt with Vegetarian Chili.

Serves 6

All this delicious medley of vegetables needs to make a complete meal is crusty bread or wholewheat rolls. For something different you might like to serve it with warmed pita bread rounds.

Tofu with Curry Sauce

3 tablespoons peanut oil
2 cloves garlic, crushed
1 tablespoon medium curry paste
1 tablespoon packed brown sugar
2 tablespoons soy sauce
1/4 cup/60 mL vegetable stock
1/2 cup/125 mL coconut milk
1 lb/500 g tofu (soy bean curd), cut into 3/4 in/2 cm cubes

Curry pastes are available from most supermarkets and all Oriental and Asian food stores.

1 Heat oil in a skillet, add garlic and cook over a medium heat for 1 minute. Stir in curry paste, sugar, soy sauce, stock and coconut milk, bring to simmering and simmer for 5 minutes or until sauce reduces and thickens slightly.

2 Arrange tofu on a serving platter, spoon sauce over and serve immediately.

Serves 4

Left: Tofu with Curry Sauce
Below: Barley and Vegetable Curry

Barley and Vegetable Curry

1/4 cup/1/2 stick/60 g butter
4 leeks, sliced
2 cloves garlic, crushed
2 teaspoons curry powder
1/2 teaspoon garam masala
1 1/2 cups/300 g pearl barley
2 large potatoes, cut into 3/4 in/2 cm cubes
12 oz/375 g butternut squash, cut into 3/4 in/2 cm cubes
4 cups/1 liter vegetable stock or water
8 oz/250 g broccoli, broken into florets

1 Melt butter in a large saucepan, add leeks and cook for 5 minutes or until soft. Stir in garlic, curry powder and garam masala and cook, stirring, for 1 minute longer.

2 Add barley, potatoes, squash and stock or water and bring to the boil. Reduce heat, cover and simmer for 15 minutes. Add broccoli and simmer for 10 minutes longer or until barley and vegetables are tender.

Serves 4

Any vegetables you wish may be used in this dish. You might like to use carrots in place of the squash, and cauliflower in place of the broccoli.

RECIPE COLLECTION

SALADS

A sensational side salad will add color, flavor and variety to an otherwise simple meal, while a more substantial salad makes a perfect one-dish main course for summer eating. For a complete meal, accompany a main course salad with crusty French bread or wholewheat rolls.

Cucumber and Fruit Salad, Apple and Watercress Salad

Cucumber and Fruit Salad

4 medium cucumbers, peeled
1/2 cantaloupe, seeds removed
1/2 honeydew melon, seeds removed
8 oz/250 g strawberries
2 tablespoons lime or lemon juice
1 tablespoon chopped fresh coriander
freshly ground black pepper

1 Using a melon baller, scoop out balls of cucumber, cantaloupe and honeydew melon. Place cucumber, melon balls and strawberries in a salad bowl.

2 Spoon lime or lemon juice over salad, sprinkle with coriander and season to taste with black pepper. Toss to combine, cover and chill for 1 hour before serving.

Serves 6

Serve this colorful salad as part of a salad selection for a buffet or barbecue. It goes particularly well with broiled or barbecued chicken.

Apple and Watercress Salad

2 green apples, cored and cut into wedges
1 bunch/250 g watercress, broken into sprigs
1/2 red onion, sliced
3 tablespoons snipped fresh chives
5 oz/155 g blue cheese, crumbled
4 tablespoons bottled French dressing

1 Place apples, watercress, onion and chives in a large bowl and toss gently to combine.

2 Sprinkle cheese over salad. Just prior to serving, drizzle dressing over salad.

Serves 4

Watercress has a peppery taste and has long been used as both a food and a medicine. It is an excellent salad vegetable whether used by itself or combined with other milder greens.

'Remember always to wash salad vegetables before using. It is best to wash salad greens as close to serving as possible.'

*Pasta and Feta Salad,
Italian Potato Salad*

Italian Potato Salad

4 lb/2 kg tiny new potatoes
10 spring onions, chopped
10 thin slices prosciutto or ham, chopped
4 oz/125 g snow pea sprouts or watercress

BLUE CHEESE MAYONNAISE
5 oz/155 g creamy blue cheese
2 tablespoons coarse grain mustard
1 cup/250 mL olive oil
freshly ground black pepper

1 Boil, steam or microwave potatoes until just tender. Drain, refresh under cold running water, then set aside to cool completely.

2 Cut cold potatoes in half. Place potatoes, spring onions and prosciutto or ham in a bowl and toss to combine.

3 To make mayonnaise, place cheese, mustard, oil and black pepper to taste in a food processor or blender and process until smooth. Spoon mayonnaise over potato mixture and toss to combine.

4 Line a large salad bowl or serving platter with snow pea sprouts or watercress, then top with potato salad.

Serves 8

A large salad that is ideal for entertaining. If this quantity is too large, simply halve the ingredients.

Pasta and Feta Salad

1 lb/500 g orrechiette or other small pasta shapes
2 tablespoons/30 g butter
1 red onion, chopped
1 cucumber, sliced
8 oz/250 g black olives
$6^1/2$ oz/200 g feta cheese, diced
freshly ground black pepper.

1 Cook pasta in boiling water in a large saucepan following package directions. Drain, set aside and keep warm.

2 Melt butter in a large skillet and cook onion over a medium heat for 4-5 minutes or until soft. Add cucumber, olives, cheese and black pepper to taste to pasta and toss to combine. Serve immediately.

Serves 6

This salad also looks attractive made with a mixture of colored pasta rather than just plain.

Warm Mussel Salad

Warm Mussel Salad

assorted lettuce leaves
1 bunch/250 g watercress
$1^1/2$ cups/375 mL dry white wine
$^1/2$ cup/125 mL water
6 spring onions, chopped
16 mussels, scrubbed and beards removed
$^1/4$ cup/60 mL walnut or vegetable oil
freshly ground black pepper
$^1/3$ cup/30 g walnut halves, coarsely chopped

1 Arrange lettuce leaves and watercress decoratively on a large serving platter.

2 Place wine, water and spring onions in a saucepan and bring to the boil. Add mussels and steam until shells open, about 5 minutes. Discard any unopened mussels. Using a slotted spoon remove mussels from liquid and arrange on lettuce bed. Strain and reserve 4 tablespoons of cooking liquid.

3 Place reserved cooking liquid, oil and black pepper to taste in a small bowl and whisk to combine. Drizzle dressing over salad, sprinkle with walnuts and serve immediately.

Serves 4

Remember, any mussels that do not open their shells when cooked should be discarded – if mussels do not open, it means that they are bad.

Italian Salad Platter

1 radicchio, leaves separated
2 large spinach leaves
1 Belgian endive, leaves separated
1 cucumber
16 green olives
8 spears canned baby sweet corn, drained

RED PEPPER AND OLIVE SALAD
1 red pepper, roasted, skinned and cut into strips
8 black olives
1 oz/30 g sun-dried tomatoes, cut into strips, or 1 tomato, peeled, seeds removed and cut into strips
1 tablespoon chopped fresh basil
freshly ground black pepper

MUSTARD DRESSING
1 clove garlic, crushed
1/2 cup/125 mL olive oil
1/4 cup/60 mL white wine vinegar
1/4 teaspoon dry mustard
pinch cayenne pepper

GRILLED CHEESE ROUNDS
8 slices bread
8 slices salami
8 slices mozzarella cheese

1 Arrange radicchio, spinach or silverbeet and Belgian endive on a large serving platter.

2 Using a vegetable peeler, peel cucumber into strips, lengthwise.

3 To make salad, place red pepper, black olives, tomatoes, basil and black pepper to taste in a bowl, toss to combine and place on platter. Arrange cucumber, salad, green olives and sweet corn on platter.

4 To make dressing, place garlic, oil, vinegar, mustard, cayenne pepper and black pepper to taste in a screwtop jar and shake well to combine. Drizzle over ingredients on platter.

5 To make Grilled Cheese Rounds, cut out 8 rounds of bread, using a large biscuit cutter. Toast bread rounds and top with a slice of salami and a slice of cheese cut to fit the bread. Place salami and cheese-topped bread rounds under a preheated broiler and cook until cheese melts. Add to platter and serve immediately.

Serves 8

Served with Italian bread, this salad platter can also make a delicious casual luncheon for four. For a complete meal, serve with a crisp dry white wine and finish with a platter of fruit or homemade ice cream.

Italian Salad Platter

Nutty Salad

1 lettuce of your choice, leaves separated
2 witloof (Belgian endive), leaves separated
$1^1/_2$ cups/155 g walnut halves, coarsely chopped

WALNUT MAYONNAISE
5 oz/155 g blue cheese, crumbled
2 tablespoons lemon juice
$^1/_2$ cup/125 mL olive oil
2 tablespoons/15 g walnut halves, ground
freshly ground black pepper

1 Place lettuce and witloof (Belgian endive) leaves and chopped walnuts in a salad bowl and toss to combine.

2 To make mayonnaise, place cheese, lemon juice, oil, ground walnuts and black pepper to taste in a food processor or blender and process until smooth. Drizzle mayonnaise over salad and serve immediately.

Serves 8

To grind walnuts, place nuts in a food processor or blender fitted with the metal blade and, using the pulse button, process until nuts are ground. Take care not to overprocess or you will end up with a nut paste.

Pears filled with Cheese Salad

1 bunch/250 g watercress, broken into small sprigs
2 pears, cored, peeled and halved
1 tablespoon lemon juice

COTTAGE CHEESE SALAD
$^1/_2$ cup/125 g cottage cheese
1 stalk celery, finely chopped
1 spring onion, finely chopped
1 tablespoon chopped fresh parsley
2 teaspoons chopped fresh tarragon or basil
2 teaspoons cider vinegar
freshly ground black pepper

1 Make a bed of watercress sprigs on a large serving platter or on individual plates. Brush pear halves with lemon juice and place, cut side uppermost, on watercress bed.

2 To make salad, place cottage cheese, celery, spring onion, parsley, tarragon or basil, vinegar and black pepper to taste in a bowl and mix to combine. Spoon salad into pear hollows and serve immediately.

Serves 4

If fresh pears are unavailable you could make this salad using canned pear halves. Drain the pear halves well and pat dry with paper towels before filling.

'Place watercress upright in a container of water, cover with a plastic bag and store in the refrigerator. For better keeping change the water daily.'

Nutty Salad,
Pears filled with Cheese Salad

SPRING SALAD

This colorful salad combines the best ingredients of spring. If asparagus is unavailable, you might like to use green beans instead.

8 oz/250 g asparagus spears, cut into $1^1/4$ in/3 cm lengths
1 bunch curly endive, leaves separated and torn into pieces
1 radicchio, leaves separated
14 oz/440 g canned artichoke hearts, drained and halved
3 carrots, cut into strips
2 hard-cooked eggs, sliced

CAPER DRESSING
$^1/4$ cup/60 mL olive oil
$^1/4$ cup/60 mL white wine vinegar
1 tablespoon chopped capers
freshly ground black pepper

1 Boil or microwave asparagus until it just changes color. Refresh under cold running water and drain well.

2 Arrange endive and radicchio leaves on a large serving platter. Top leaves with asparagus, artichoke hearts, carrots and eggs.

3 To make dressing, place oil, vinegar, capers and black pepper to taste in a screwtop jar and shake well to combine. Drizzle over salad and serve immediately.

Serves 4

CHILI SHRIMP SALAD

A salad such as this one is a wonderful way of making a few shrimp go a long way. Remember salads can be a great way of stretching the budget and cutting down on your consumption of animal foods.

1 lettuce of your choice, leaves separated and torn into pieces
16 large cooked shrimp, shelled and deveined, tails left intact
1 onion, sliced into rings
4 oz/125 g cherry tomatoes
1 carrot, cut into slices, then into eighths
1 red pepper, cut into strips
1 tablespoon chopped fresh parsley

CHILI DRESSING
2 tablespoons lemon juice
2 tablespoons olive oil
$^1/4$ teaspoon chili paste (sambal oelek)
freshly ground black pepper

1 Line a large serving platter with lettuce leaves. Arrange shrimp, onion, tomatoes, carrot and red pepper attractively on lettuce bed.

2 To make dressing, place lemon juice, oil, chili paste (sambal oelek) and black pepper to taste in a screwtop jar and shake well to combine. Just prior to serving, drizzle dressing over salad and sprinkle with parsley. Serve immediately.

Serves 4

Chili Shrimp Salad, Spring Salad

Chicken Potato Salad

Quick to prepare and sure to please, this substantial salad needs no other accompaniment. For the very hungry you might like to serve a salad of tossed assorted lettuces and fresh herbs, and thick slices of wholewheat bread. Fill pocket bread with leftover salad for a delicious lunch the next day.

8 oz/250 g cooked chicken, skin removed, flesh cut into bite-sized pieces
4 zucchini, shredded
1 teaspoon chopped fresh thyme or 1/4 teaspoon dried thyme
8 tiny new potatoes, cooked and halved
1 red pepper, cut into strips
4 hard-cooked eggs, sliced
1 tablespoon chopped fresh coriander or parsley

CREAMY DRESSING

1/4 cup/60 mL bottled French dressing
2 tablespoons mayonnaise
freshly ground black pepper

1 Place chicken, zucchini, thyme and potatoes in a bowl and toss to combine.

2 Divide chicken mixture between serving plates and top with red pepper and eggs.

3 To make dressing, place French dressing, mayonnaise and black pepper to taste in a small bowl and whisk to combine. Drizzle dressing over salad and sprinkle with coriander or parsley.

Serves 4

Above: Tuna and Olive Salad
Left: Chicken Potato Salad

Tuna and Olive Salad

1 bunch curly endive, leaves separated
1 romaine lettuce, leaves separated
4 oz/125 g cherry tomatoes, halved
5 oz/155 g green beans, trimmed and blanched
8 tiny new potatoes, cooked and halved
3 hard-cooked eggs, quartered
4 spring onions, chopped
1/2 red pepper, cut into strips
1/2 green pepper, cut into strips
12 black olives
14 oz/440 g canned tuna, drained and flaked
3 tablespoons chopped fresh parsley

ANCHOVY DRESSING

1 clove garlic, crushed
4 anchovy fillets, drained
freshly ground black pepper
1/4 teaspoon sugar
2 teaspoons finely chopped fresh basil
2 tablespoons cider vinegar
4 tablespoons olive oil

1 Arrange endive and romaine in a large salad bowl. Place tomatoes, beans, potatoes, eggs, spring onions, red and green peppers, olives, tuna and parsley in a separate bowl and toss gently to combine. Arrange tuna mixture attractively over lettuce.

2 To make dressing, place garlic, anchovy fillets, black pepper to taste, sugar, basil, vinegar and oil in a food processor or blender and process to combine. Drizzle dressing over salad and serve immediately.

Serves 4

A variation on the traditional Salad Niçoise, this is another salad that only requires fresh bread to make a complete meal. For a healthy choice, choose tuna canned in water rather than oil.

Curried Chicken Salad

Use a purchased French dressing or make your own for this recipe. See the Dressings chapter for a recipe. Either the Fast French Dressing or the Light Vinaigrette would be suitable.

1 bunch/250 g watercress, broken into sprigs
1 cooked chicken, skin removed and flesh torn into pieces
10 oz/315 g canned pineapple pieces, drained
$^2/_3$ cup/60 g walnut halves
4 cherry tomatoes, halved

CURRIED DRESSING

$^1/_4$ cup/60 mL bottled French dressing
2 teaspoons mild curry powder
freshly ground black pepper

1 Arrange watercress, chicken, pineapple, walnuts and tomatoes on a large serving platter or individual serving plates.

2 To make dressing, place French dressing, curry powder and black pepper to taste in a screwtop jar and shake well to combine. Just prior to serving, spoon dressing over salad.

Serves 6

Tofu and Broccoli Salad

Tofu or bean curd has less than 5 per cent fat, no cholesterol and virtually no sodium (salt). It is a good source of protein, minerals and B-group vitamins and a great food for weight watchers, the cholesterol-conscious and vegetarians.

1 large head broccoli, broken into florets
$6^1/_2$ oz/200 g tofu, drained and cut into $^3/_4$ in/2 cm cubes
1 red pepper, cut into $^1/_2$ in/1 cm squares

PEANUT SAUCE

3 tablespoons smooth peanut butter
$^1/_2$ cup/125 mL whipping cream
$^1/_4$ cup/60 mL water

1 Boil, steam or microwave broccoli until it just changes color. Refresh under cold running water and drain well. Place broccoli, tofu and red pepper in a salad bowl and toss gently to combine.

2 To make sauce, place peanut butter in a small saucepan and cook over a low heat, stirring, for 1-2 minutes or until just warm. Stir in half the cream and cook, stirring, for 2-3 minutes longer or until combined. Remove pan from heat and stir in water and remaining cream. Spoon sauce over salad and serve immediately.

Serves 4

Curried Chicken Salad,
Tofu and Broccoli Salad

Three-Cabbage Hot Slaw

Sesame oil has a distinctive nutty flavor and is often used in Asian cooking. It is available from Asian food stores and some supermarkets. Care should be taken when using sesame oil, as a little adds a lot of taste.

1 tablespoon vegetable oil
1 teaspoon sesame oil
1 clove garlic, crushed
1 teaspoon grated fresh ginger
1 red chili, seeds removed and chopped
1 tablespoon sesame seeds
1/4 red cabbage, shredded
1/4 Chinese cabbage, shredded
1/4 savoy cabbage, shredded

1 Heat vegetable and sesame oils in a wok or skillet and stir-fry garlic, ginger, chili and sesame seeds for 1 minute.

2 Toss in red, Chinese and savoy cabbages and stir-fry for 3-4 minutes or until just cooked. The cabbages should still retain their colors and be crisp. Serve immediately.

Serves 6

Marinated Eggplant Salad

If the eggplant slices appear to be drying out during cooking, brush with a little more olive oil. This salad is even better if left to marinate overnight. It is also delicious served as a starter, as part of an antipasto platter, taken on a picnic or served with pita bread and plain yogurt.

6 baby eggplant, cut lengthwise into 1/2 in/1 cm slices or
2 eggplant, cut crosswise into 1/2 in/1 cm slices
olive oil
3 tomatoes, peeled and thinly sliced
4 tablespoons chopped fresh basil
freshly ground black pepper

BALSAMIC DRESSING

3 tablespoons balsamic or red wine vinegar
1 tablespoon olive oil
2 cloves garlic, crushed

1 Brush each eggplant slice generously with olive oil and cook under a preheated broiler for 4-5 minutes each side or until golden and tender.

2 To make dressing, place vinegar, oil and garlic in a screwtop jar and shake well to combine.

3 Place a layer of warm eggplant slices in a shallow ceramic or glass dish. Top with a layer of tomato slices. Sprinkle with a tablespoon of dressing, a tablespoon of basil and season with black pepper. Repeat layers until all eggplant and tomatoes are used. Cover and refrigerate for at least 2 hours.

Serves 6

Couscous Salad

Couscous Salad

1 cup/250 mL chicken stock or water
6$^{1}/_{2}$ oz/200 g couscous
1 carrot, thinly sliced
1 red pepper, chopped
1 tomato, chopped
1 small cucumber, cubed
1 avocado, pitted, peeled and cubed
$^{1}/_{4}$ cup/30 g sliced almonds, toasted

LIME AND MUSTARD DRESSING
1 tablespoon olive oil
1 teaspoon finely grated lime peel
2 tablespoons lime juice
1 teaspoon coarse grain mustard
1 tablespoon honey
1 tablespoon chopped fresh basil
freshly ground black pepper

1 Place stock or water in a saucepan and bring to the boil. Place couscous in a bowl. Pour boiling stock or water over couscous and set aside to stand for 10 minutes or until couscous absorbs the liquid.

2 Place couscous, carrot, red pepper, tomato, cucumber and avocado in a salad bowl.

3 To make dressing, place oil, lime peel, lime juice, mustard, honey, basil and black pepper to taste in a screwtop jar and shake well to combine. Spoon dressing over salad and toss gently. Just prior to serving, sprinkle salad with almonds.

Serves 4

Couscous is a fine semolina made from wheat. It originated in North Africa; however, variations on the traditional dish can be found in Sicily, France and even Brazil, where it is *cuscuz* rather than couscous. The name 'couscous' applies to both the uncooked granules and the finished dish.

Warm Oriental Chicken Salad

Warm Oriental Chicken Salad

The best way to cook a chicken for a chicken salad is to place it breast side down in a saucepan. Pour over enough cold water just to cover the bird. Cut 1 onion into thick slices and add to pan with 4 peppercorns and several sprigs of parsley. Bring to the boil over a medium heat, then reduce heat, cover and simmer for 45 minutes or until chicken is cooked. Transfer chicken and cooking liquid to a large bowl. Ensure that chicken is breast side down in the bowl so that the breast flesh remains moist. Cover and refrigerate until cold.

7 oz/220 g cellophane or transparent noodles
boiling water
1 cooked chicken, skin removed and flesh shredded
1 carrot, shredded
3 tablespoons chopped fresh coriander
1 cucumber, chopped
3 tablespoons/30 g peanuts, chopped

PEANUT DRESSING

2 cloves garlic, crushed
1/4 cup/60 mL soy sauce
1/4 cup/60 mL fresh lemon juice
1 tablespoon peanut butter
1/3 cup/90 mL vegetable oil
1 tablespoon packed brown sugar

1 Place noodles in a large heatproof bowl, pour over boiling water to cover and set aside to stand for 10 minutes. Drain.

2 Place chicken, carrot, coriander and cucumber in a bowl and mix to combine.

3 To make dressing, place garlic, soy sauce, lemon juice, peanut butter, oil and sugar in a small saucepan and bring to the boil, stirring, over a medium heat. Cook, stirring, for 3 minutes. Pour dressing over chicken and toss to combine.

4 Divide noodles between four plates, top with chicken mixture and sprinkle with peanuts. Serve immediately.

Serves 4 as a main meal

Chicken and Orange Salad

1 cooked chicken, skin removed and flesh cut into bite-sized pieces
2 stalks celery, sliced
7 oz/220 g canned water chestnuts, drained and halved
1 orange, segmented
1 red onion, chopped

TARRAGON DRESSING
1 tablespoon chopped fresh parsley
1/3 cup/90 mL safflower oil
1 clove garlic, crushed
1/4 cup/60 mL tarragon vinegar

1 Place chicken, celery, water chestnuts, orange segments and onion in a salad bowl. Toss gently to combine.

2 To make dressing, place parsley, oil, garlic and vinegar in a screwtop jar, and shake well to combine. Pour over salad and toss gently.

Serves 4

Chunks of tender chicken, pieces of crunchy celery and water chestnuts team with fresh-tasting orange segments to make the perfect summer lunch.

Chicken and Orange Salad

Spinach and Chicken Liver Salad

6 slices white bread, crusts removed
1/4 cup/1/2 stick/60 g butter
8 oz/250 g chicken livers, trimmed
3 tablespoons brandy
1 tablespoon dried mixed herbs
8 oz/250 g fresh spinach, stalks removed and discarded
1/4 cup/60 mL dry white wine
1 tablespoon olive oil
1 red pepper, finely chopped

Serves 4 as a starter or light meal

1 Using cookie cutters, cut bread into decorative shapes. Melt half the butter in a skillet over a medium heat until bubbling. Add bread and cook for 1-2 minutes each side or until golden. Remove croutons from pan and drain on paper towels.

2 Melt remaining butter in skillet and cook chicken livers, stirring constantly, for 2-3 minutes. Add brandy and herbs and cook for 3 minutes longer.

3 Arrange spinach on a large platter or in a salad bowl. Using a slotted spoon remove chicken livers from pan, slice and scatter over spinach. Add wine to pan and cook over a medium heat for 2 minutes, strain mixture into small bowl and discard any sediment. Add oil to strained mixture and mix to combine. Spoon dressing over salad, then top with croutons and red pepper.

Warm chicken livers, pretty-shaped croutons and spinach combine to make an attractive starter.

Spinach and Chicken Liver Salad

Creamy Roast Duck Salad

1 x 4 lb/2 kg duck
freshly ground black pepper
2 tablespoons chopped fresh parsley

CREAMY ONION DRESSING
2 red onions, cut into wedges
2 tablespoons vegetable oil
3/4 cup/185 mL chicken stock
1/2 cup/125 mL dry white wine
3/4 cup/185 g dairy sour cream

1 Season duck with black pepper. Tuck wings under body of duck and tie legs together. Place bird breast side up on a wire rack set in a baking pan and bake for 1 hour or until duck is cooked. Remove from pan and set aside to cool completely.

2 To make dressing, separate onion wedges. Heat oil in a skillet and cook onions for 5 minutes or until soft. Stir in stock and cook for 8 minutes. Add wine, bring to the boil, then reduce heat and simmer for 5 minutes, stirring to lift sediment from base of pan. Remove pan from heat, transfer contents to a bowl and set aside to cool to room temperature. Place sour cream in a bowl, add stock mixture and mix well to combine.

3 Remove skin from duck and discard. Strip flesh from duck, cut into bite-sized pieces and place in a bowl. Add dressing and toss to combine. Just prior to serving, sprinkle with parsley. Serve salad at room temperature or chilled.

Serves 4 as a light meal

Oven temperature
350°F, 180°C

Serve this delicious duck salad with boiled new potatoes or a plain rice dish and cold asparagus spears.

Creamy Roast Duck Salad

Potato and Egg Salad

If hard-cooked eggs are overcooked, a dark ring will form around the yolk. This is because the iron in the egg yolk combines with the sulphur in the egg white and the result is a greyish-black iron sulphide ring. To prevent this, avoid overcooking eggs and cool the unshelled cooked eggs quickly in cold water.

2 lb/1 kg tiny, new potatoes, scrubbed
2 tablespoons chopped fresh parsley
6 hard-cooked eggs, quartered
1 onion, thinly sliced

AVOCADO DRESSING

1 avocado, pitted, peeled and chopped
1 clove garlic, crushed
1 tablespoon lemon juice
1/2 cup/125 g dairy sour cream or plain yogurt
2 drops bottled hot pepper seasoning
1 teaspoon honey

1 Boil, steam or microwave potatoes until just tender. Drain and refresh under cold running water. Place potatoes, parsley, eggs and onion in a large salad bowl.

2 To make dressing, place avocado, garlic, lemon juice, sour cream or yogurt, pepper seasoning and honey in a food processor or blender and process until smooth. Just prior to serving, spoon dressing over salad.

Serves 6

Potato and Egg Salad

Carpaccio

CARPACCIO

1 lb/500 g rib eye (Delmonico) steak, in one piece
1 lettuce, leaves separated and washed
1 bunch 8 oz/250 g watercress
$^{3}/_{4}$ cup/90 g Parmesan cheese, grated

MUSTARD MAYONNAISE
1 egg
1 tablespoon lemon juice
2 cloves garlic, crushed
2 teaspoons Dijon mustard
$^{1}/_{2}$ cup/125 mL olive oil
freshly ground black pepper

1 Trim meat of all visible fat and cut into wafer-thin slices. Arrange beef slices, lettuce leaves and watercress attractively on four serving plates. Sprinkle with Parmesan cheese.

2 To make mayonnaise, place egg, lemon juice, garlic and mustard in a food processor or blender and process to combine. With machine running, slowly add oil and continue processing until mayonnaise thickens. Season to taste with black pepper. Spoon a little mayonnaise over salad and serve immediately.

Serves 4

To achieve very thin slices of beef, wrap the steak in plastic wrap and place in the freezer for 15 minutes or until firm, then slice using a very sharp knife.

Tossed Egg Salad

Tossed Egg Salad

1 lettuce, leaves separated and washed
10 stuffed green olives, halved
5 black olives, pitted and sliced
4 hard-cooked eggs, sliced
1 red pepper, cut into thin strips
2 stalks celery, cut into thin strips

HONEY DRESSING

2 tablespoons red wine vinegar
1 teaspoon honey
1 tablespoon lime juice
1 teaspoon olive oil

1 Arrange lettuce, green and black olives, eggs, red pepper and celery on a large platter.

2 To make dressing, place vinegar, honey, lime juice and oil in a screwtop jar and shake well to combine. Drizzle over salad and serve immediately.

Serves 4 as a light meal

Ideal for weight watchers, this salad is an elegant lunch or supper dish. For a complete meal, accompany with crusty bread and finish with a piece of fresh fruit.

Mozzarella and Egg Salad

Mozzarella and Egg Salad

$9^1/2$ oz/300 g mozzarella cheese, cut into $^3/4$ in/2 cm batons
1 bunch/8 oz/250 g watercress, broken into small sprigs
8 hard-cooked quail's eggs, halved

CREAMY DRESSING
$^1/4$ cup/60 mL whipping cream
3 tablespoons mayonnaise
2 tablespoons white wine vinegar
freshly ground black pepper

1 To make dressing, place cream, mayonnaise, vinegar and black pepper to taste in a bowl and whisk to combine. Add cheese batons to dressing and toss to coat.

2 Arrange watercress sprigs on individual serving plates or a large serving platter. Top with cheese and quail's eggs and serve immediately.

Serves 4

If quail's eggs are unavailable, this salad is just as delicious made with hen's eggs. Use 4 hen's eggs, hard-cooked and cut into quarters, in place of the quail's eggs.

Potato Knackwurst Salad

Oven temperature
425°F/220°C

1 lb/500 g tiny new potatoes, peeled and halved
3 tablespoons vegetable oil
4 Knackwurst or Polish sausages
3 spring onions, chopped

CHIVE DRESSING
2 tablespoons snipped fresh chives
1 clove garlic, crushed
2 teaspoons lemon juice
1/4 cup/45 g plain yogurt
1/4 cup/60 g dairy sour cream
freshly ground black pepper

1 Boil or microwave potatoes until just tender. Drain, then toss in 2 tablespoons oil. Place in a baking pan and bake, turning occasionally, for 20 minutes or until golden.

2 Heat remaining oil in a skillet and cook sausages until golden and cooked through. Remove from pan, drain on paper towels, allow to cool then cut into slices.

3 Add asparagus and spring onions to skillet and stir-fry for 2-3 minutes or until asparagus changes color and is just tender. Drain and set aside to cool. Place potatoes, sausages and asparagus mixture in a bowl and toss gently to combine.

4 To make dressing, place chives, garlic, lemon juice, yogurt, sour cream and black pepper to taste in a food processor or blender and process until smooth.

Serves 4

To serve, divide salad between four plates and spoon over dressing. While this is a complete meal, you might also like to serve crusty bread or rolls for very hungry people. Knackwurst or Polish sausages are available from continental delicatessens and some butchers.

Coriander Beef Salad

1 lb/500 g sirloin steak
1 bunch 8oz/250 g watercress or 1 lettuce
1/2 red pepper, cut into thin strips

CORIANDER DRESSING
2 cloves garlic, crushed
4 tablespoons chopped fresh coriander
3 tablespoons chopped fresh mint leaves
2 tablespoons olive oil
1 teaspoon chili paste (sambal oelek)
2 tablespoons lime juice
2 teaspoons bottled fish sauce
2 teaspoons packed brown sugar
1/2 teaspoon ground cumin
freshly ground black pepper

1 Cook steak under a preheated broiler for 3-4 minutes each side or until medium rare. Remove steak from broiler and set aside to cool. Cut cold steak into slices across the grain.

2 To make dressing, place garlic, coriander, mint, oil, chili paste (sambal oelek), lime juice, fish sauce, sugar, cumin and black pepper to taste in a food processor or blender and process to combine.

3 Arrange watercress, or lettuce, and steak on a serving platter, drizzle dressing over and garnish with red pepper strips.

Serves 4

Coriander is a herb you either love or hate. If you fall into the second category you could make this salad using parsley in place of the coriander.

Potato Knackwurst Salad,
Coriander Beef Salad

SNACKS

Today's lifestyles and the trend towards 'grazing', or snacking, demand a variety of recipes that take only minutes to create. The recipes in this chapter fit the bill perfectly and many are also suitable for a special brunch or supper.

Smoked Salmon Bagels

Smoked Salmon Bagels

4 oz/125 g cream cheese
4 tablespoons dairy sour cream
1 small onion, finely chopped
2 tablespoons chopped fresh parsley
1 tablespoon chopped capers
2 tablespoons lemon juice
freshly ground black pepper
8 bagels, split
1 bunch/8 oz/250 g watercress
8 oz/250 g sliced smoked salmon

1 Place cream cheese and sour cream in a small bowl and beat to combine. Stir in onion, parsley, capers, lemon juice and black pepper to taste.

2 Spread top half of each bagel with cream cheese mixture. Place watercress and salmon on each bottom half then cover with top half of bagel.

Makes 8

A bagel is a traditional Jewish roll. It is ring-shaped and is cooked twice. Cooking involves boiling first, for about 15 seconds, then the bagel is baked.

Vegetable and Salmon Souffles

$^{1}/_{2}$ cup/125 g dairy sour cream or plain yogurt
1 teaspoon chili sauce
7 oz/220 g canned pink salmon, drained and flaked
2 eggs, separated
freshly ground black pepper
2 large zucchini, shredded

1 Place sour cream or yogurt, chili sauce, salmon, egg yolks and black pepper to taste in a food processor or blender and process to combine. Stir in zucchini.

2 Place egg whites in a bowl and beat until stiff peaks form. Fold egg whites into salmon mixture. Spoon soufflé mixture into four $1^{1}/_{2}$ cup/375 mL capacity soufflé dishes and bake for 25 minutes or until soufflés are puffed and golden.

Serves 4

Oven temperature
400°F, 200°C

Mostly sold vacuum-packed, smoked salmon will keep in the refrigerator for about 10 days once opened. It also keeps well in the freezer. Smoked salmon should be pink-orange in color, moist and with a mild smoky smell and delicate flavor.

'Fish is an important source of protein and contains many important minerals such as magnesium, iron, iodine and selenium.'

Lamb and Onion Rolls

6 long rolls, split horizontally
1 lb/500 g cold roast lamb, sliced
2 oz/60 g alfalfa sprouts

SWEET AND SOUR ONION RELISH
2 large red onions, sliced
2 spring onions, chopped
2 tablespoons/30 g golden raisins
2 tablespoons oil
1/4 cup/45 g packed brown sugar
1/4 cup/60 mL cider vinegar
freshly ground black pepper

1 To make relish, place onions, spring onions, raisins and oil in saucepan, cover and cook over a low heat, stirring occasionally, for 30 minutes or until onions are golden and very tender. Stir in sugar, vinegar and black pepper to taste and cook, uncovered, for 30 minutes longer or until almost all the moisture has evaporated. Remove pan from heat and set aside to cool.

2 Top bottom half of each roll with lamb slices, alfalfa sprouts, some onion relish and finally the top of roll.

Serves 6

Any leftover relish will keep in the refrigerator for 2-3 weeks and is delicious with cold meat or cheese.

Marinated Feta Salad

2 cups/500 mL olive oil
2 tablespoons dried oregano
2 cloves garlic, thinly sliced
1 lb/500 g feta cheese, cut into 3/4 in/2 cm cubes
12 black olives
1 red pepper, roasted, skinned and sliced
4 sprigs fresh oregano

1 Place oil, dried oregano and half the garlic in a large saucepan and cook over a low heat for 10 minutes or until warmed. Remove pan from heat and set aside to cool.

2 Place cheese, olives, red pepper, fresh oregano sprigs and remaining garlic in a large sterilized jar. Strain oil mixture and discard solids. Pour oil over ingredients in jar, seal and refrigerate for at least 2 days before using.

Serves 6

The flavor of this Marinated Feta Salad is best when served at room temperature. It makes a delicious meal served with crusty bread or wholewheat rolls.

Lamb and Onion Rolls,
Marinated Feta Salad

Right: Mini Pizza Triangles
Far right: Grilled Goat's Cheese Toast

Mini Pizza Triangles

Oven temperature
350°F, 180°C

Children will love these crisp pizza triangles. Serve them hot as an after-school snack, warm at birthday parties and cold in packed lunches. And, of course, the toppings can be changed to suit individual tastes.

4 pita bread rounds
1 cup/250 mL prepared tomato pasta sauce
1 green pepper, chopped
1 red onion, chopped
7 oz/220 g small shrimp, shelled or 4 oz/125 g canned shrimp, drained
3 tablespoons chopped pineapple pieces
4 oz/125 g salami, chopped
$3^1/2$ oz /100 g button mushrooms, sliced
1 cup/125 g shredded mozzarella cheese

1 Spread each pita bread round with tomato pasta sauce, then top with green pepper and onion.

2 Top two pita bread rounds with shrimp and pineapple. Top the remaining two with salami and mushrooms. Sprinkle pizzas with cheese and bake for 20 minutes or until cheese is melted and bread is crisp. Cut into triangles and serve.

Serves 8

Grilled Goat's Cheese Toast

1 radicchio, leaves separated
8 cherry tomatoes, halved
$^1/_2$ bunch/4 oz/125 g watercress, broken into small sprigs
1 clove garlic, crushed
$3^1/_2$ oz/100 g goat's cheese
2 oz/60 g light cream cheese
freshly ground black pepper
8 slices bread, crusts trimmed

1 Arrange radicchio, tomatoes and watercress on individual serving plates.

2 Place garlic, goat's cheese, cream cheese and black pepper to taste in a bowl and mix to combine. Set aside.

3 Toast bread slices, then spread with cheese mixture. Place under a preheated broiler and cook for 2-3 minutes or until cheese mixture is golden. Cut toast in half diagonally and place 4 pieces on each salad. Serve immediately.

Serves 4

These cheese toasts are delicious made with rye or grain bread.

Cheese and Garlic Crisps

Oven temperature
350°F, 180°C

The crisps will keep in an airtight container for up to a week and are great to have on hand for after-school or work snacks.

4 pita bread rounds
$^1/_2$ cup/1 stick/125 g butter, melted
3 cloves garlic, crushed
2 tablespoons chopped fresh basil
4 tablespoons grated Parmesan cheese

1 Split each pita bread round in half, horizontally, then cut each half into four wedges.

2 Place butter, garlic and basil in a bowl and mix to combine. Place pita wedges cut side up on a lightly oiled baking sheet. Brush each pita wedge with butter mixture then sprinkle with Parmesan cheese and bake for 10 minutes or until golden and crisp.

Makes 32 wedges

Left: Cheese and Garlic Crisps
Below: Turkey and Stilton Sandwiches

Turkey and Stilton Sandwiches

1 French baguette, cut into 12 thick slices
2 tablespoons Dijon mustard
12 slices smoked turkey
$6^1/2$ oz/200 g Stilton cheese, crumbled
1 oz/30 g watercress, broken into sprigs

Spread each slice of bread with mustard. Top with turkey and cheese and garnish with watercress. Serve immediately.

Serves 6

Every country seems to have its own favorite blue cheese. Stilton is the blue cheese of Britain. For these sandwiches you can choose your favorite blue cheese. If you do not like blue cheese you might like to use Brie, Camembert or a cream cheese instead.

Mini Carrot and Feta Quiches

Oven temperature
350°F, 180°C

Traditionally made from sheep's milk, feta cheese is crumbly and dripping with whey when fresh, but as it matures it becomes dry and somewhat salty.

1 lb/500 g prerolled frozen puff pastry sheets

CARROT AND FETA FILLING

4 slices bacon, finely chopped
4 spring onions, chopped
2 carrots, shredded
4 oz/125 g feta cheese, crumbled
3 eggs
1 cup/250 mL milk
1 cup/125 g shredded mature Cheddar cheese
freshly ground black pepper

1 To make filling, cook bacon and spring onions in a skillet over a medium heat for 4-5 minutes or until bacon is crisp. Add carrots and cook, stirring, for 2-3 minutes longer. Remove pan from heat and set aside to cool.

2 Place feta cheese, eggs, milk, Cheddar and black pepper to taste in a bowl and mix to combine. Stir in carrot mixture and set aside.

3 Using a 2$^{1}/_{2}$-3 in/6-7.5 cm scalloped cookie or biscuit cutter, cut out 24 rounds from pastry sheets. Place rounds in lightly greased, shallow muffin or cupcake pans. Divide filling between pastry shells and bake for 15-20 minutes or until pastry is golden and filling is set.

Makes 24

Below: Health Club Sandwiches

Health Club Sandwiches

2 tablespoons/30 g butter
4 slices multiwheat bread
4 slices rye bread
1/2 bunch curly endive, leaves separated
4 slices lean ham
2 tomatoes, sliced
4 slices pumpernickel
4 slices mature Cheddar cheese
1/2 bunch/4 oz/125 g watercress
freshly ground black pepper

1 Spread butter thinly on one side of each slice of multiwheat and rye bread. Top rye bread with endive leaves, ham and tomatoes, then slices of pumpernickel.

2 Place cheese and watercress on pumpernickel, season to taste with black pepper and top with multiwheat bread. Cut each sandwich in half and serve immediately.

Serves 4

These sandwiches are also delicious made with cold lean roast beef, lamb or pork, cooked chicken or canned salmon in place of the ham. You might also like to try different types of lettuce and for a vegetarian sandwich shredded carrot or sweet corn kernels are delicious.

Peaches and Cream Muffins

Recognized as the dieter's cheese, cottage cheese is made from skim milk and so has a fat content of only 3 per cent. Like ricotta it is one of the great cooking cheeses and is widely used in cheesecakes.

4 tablespoons cottage cheese
pulp of 1 passion fruit or 1 tablespoon passion fruit pulp
2 English muffins, split and toasted
2 peaches, pitted and sliced

Place cottage cheese and passion fruit pulp in a small bowl and mix to combine. Spread mixture over muffin halves, top with peach slices and serve immediately.

Serves 2

Fruit and Nut Muffins

Why not try these muffins as a special breakfast treat? If you do not have ricotta cheese, use cottage cheese in its place.

4 tablespoons ricotta cheese
1 tablespoon dried currants
1 tablespoon chopped raisins
1 teaspoon finely grated orange peel
2 English muffins, split and toasted
2 tablespoons chopped pecans or walnuts

Place ricotta cheese, currants, raisins and orange rind in a small bowl and mix to combine. Spread over muffin halves and sprinkle with pecans. Serve immediately.

Serves 2

Turkey and Cheese Muffins

2 English muffins, split and toasted
1 tomato, sliced
4 thin slices cooked turkey breast
3 tablespoons shredded mature Cheddar cheese
freshly ground black pepper

Top each muffin half with tomato, turkey, cheese and black pepper to taste and cook under a preheated broiler for 2-3 minutes or until cheese melts.

Serves 2

Peaches and Cream Muffins, Fruit and Nut Muffins, Turkey and Cheese Muffins

Seafood Kabobs

Remember to soak bamboo skewers in cold water for an hour or so before threading with food. This prevents them from splintering and burning during cooking. Lightly oil the skewers after soaking, this prevents the food from sticking and makes it easy to remove when eating.

8 scallops
2 x 4 oz/125 g firm white fish fillets, cut into eight squares
8 cooked shrimp, shelled and deveined

BASIL AND CHIVE BUTTER

1/2 cup/1 stick/125 g butter, softened
2 tablespoons chopped fresh basil
2 tablespoons snipped fresh chives
1 tablespoon lemon juice
freshly ground black pepper

1 To make Basil and Chive Butter, place butter, basil, chives, lemon juice and black pepper to taste in a bowl and beat to combine.

2 Thread a scallop, a piece of fish and a shrimp onto a lightly oiled bamboo skewer. Repeat with remaining seafood to make eight kabobs. Spread each kabob with a little butter and cook under a preheated broiler, basting frequently for 3-4 minutes each side or until scallops and fish are cooked.

Serves 4

Salmon Salad Roll-Ups

Weight watchers might like to make these roll-ups using low-fat cottage or ricotta cheese instead of cream cheese.

8 oz/250 g cream cheese
2 tablespoons snipped fresh chives
2 tablespoons lemon juice
freshly ground black pepper
4 pita bread rounds
shredded lettuce
1/4 red pepper, sliced
1/4 green pepper, sliced
1 onion, chopped
14 oz/440 g canned pink salmon, drained and flaked

1 Place cream cheese, chives, lemon juice and black pepper to taste in a bowl and beat to combine.

2 Spread each pita bread with cream cheese mixture, then top with lettuce, red and green pepper, onion and salmon. Roll up tightly, secure with wooden toothpicks and serve immediately or wrap in plastic wrap for a packed lunch.

Serves 4

'Fatty fish, such as tuna, salmon, sardines, herring and mackerel, have the highest levels of Omega-3.'

Seafood Kabobs,
Vegetable and Salmon Soufflés,
Salmon Salad Roll-Ups

Right: Egg and Salmon Sandwiches
Below: Salmon Croquettes

Salmon Croquettes

3 large potatoes, cooked and mashed
1 onion, grated
14 oz/440 g canned pink salmon, drained and flaked
1 teaspoon Dijon mustard
2 tablespoons mayonnaise
1 egg, beaten
freshly ground black pepper
$6^{1}/_{2}$ oz/200 g cheese-flavored crackers, crushed
vegetable oil for deep-frying

1 Place potatoes, onion, salmon, mustard, mayonnaise, egg and black pepper to taste in a bowl and mix well to combine. Shape mixture into croquettes and roll in crushed crackers to coat. Place croquettes on a plate lined with plastic wrap and refrigerate for 15 minutes.

2 Heat oil in a large deep saucepan until a cube of bread dropped into it browns in 50 seconds. Add croquettes and cook over a medium heat for 4-5 minutes or until golden. Drain on paper towels and serve immediately.

Serves 4

These croquettes are great to have on hand for snacks and quick meals. After cooking, the croquettes can be frozen then all you need to do is reheat them in the oven at 350°F/180°C for 15-20 minutes or until heated through.

Egg and Salmon Sandwiches

8 eggs
1/4 cup/60 mL whipping cream
1 tablespoon snipped fresh chives
freshly ground black pepper
1/4 cup/1/2 stick/60 g butter
4 slices bread
4 slices smoked salmon

1 Place eggs, cream, chives and black pepper to taste in a bowl and whisk to combine. Melt butter in a saucepan, add egg mixture and cook over a low heat, stirring gently, until egg mixture is set but still creamy.

2 Top each slice of bread with a slice of salmon, then with scrambled eggs. Serve immediately.

Serves 4

Keep this rather rich dish for a special brunch or supper dish. In place of the bread you might like to use a split bagel or a split, toasted English muffin.

RECIPE COLLECTION

ACCOMPANIMENTS

An otherwise simple meal becomes something special when served with interesting side dishes. The inspiring recipes in this chapter show you ways to create wonderfully delicious side dishes.

Spiced Broccoli Pilau

Spiced Broccoli Pilau

1/4 cup/1/2 stick/60 g butter
1 onion, chopped
1 clove garlic, crushed
1 tablespoon cumin seeds
2 cinnamon sticks
2 bay leaves
1 teaspoon ground cardamom
1 head broccoli, broken into small florets
1/3 cup/90 mL water
1 1/2 cups/330 g basmati rice, cooked
3/4 cup/125 g roasted cashews
2 oranges, segmented

1 Melt butter in a large skillet, add onion and cook for 4-5 minutes or until onion is soft. Stir in garlic, cumin seeds, cinnamon, bay leaves and cardamom and cook for 1 minute.

2 Add broccoli and water, cover and cook for 5 minutes or until broccoli is tender.

3 Stir in rice, cashews and oranges and cook for 5 minutes longer or until heated through.

Serves 6

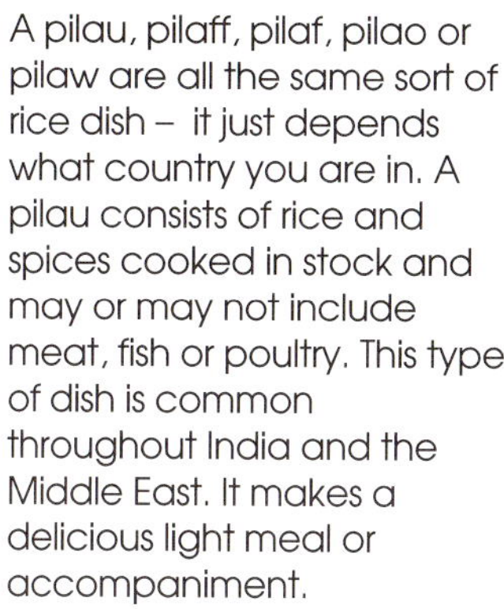
A pilau, pilaff, pilaf, pilao or pilaw are all the same sort of rice dish – it just depends what country you are in. A pilau consists of rice and spices cooked in stock and may or may not include meat, fish or poultry. This type of dish is common throughout India and the Middle East. It makes a delicious light meal or accompaniment.

Rose-scented Saffron Rice

2 1/2 cups/500 g basmati rice, washed
1/4 cup/60 g ghee or clarified butter
1 onion, chopped
8 oz/250 g lean ground lamb
1/2 teaspoon pumpkin pie spice
1/3 cup/60 g dried currants
1/2 teaspoon powdered saffron
2 tablespoons bottled rosewater
4 cups/1 liter chicken stock
1/3 cup/60 g blanched almonds, toasted

1 Place rice in a large bowl, cover with cold water and set aside to stand for 30 minutes.

2 Heat ghee or butter in a large heavy-based skillet over a medium heat, add onion and cook for 5 minutes or until soft. Increase heat, add lamb and cook until browned. Stir in pie spice and currants and cook for 1 minute longer. Remove pan from heat, set aside and keep warm.

3 Place saffron and rosewater in a cup and mix to combine. Place chicken stock and 2 teaspoons rosewater mixture in a large saucepan and bring to the boil. Drain rice, add to stock mixture and bring back to the boil, stirring occasionally. Reduce heat, cover and simmer for 30 minutes.

4 Mix meat mixture into rice, remove pan from heat, cover and set aside to stand for 5 minutes before serving. To serve, sprinkle with remaining rosewater mixture and top with almonds.

Serves 6

To clarify butter, place it in a small saucepan and melt it over a low heat. Skim the foam from the surface of the butter, then slowly pour the butter into a bowl, leaving behind the milky-white solids. Ghee is a type of clarified butter.

Pilau with Vegetables

Pilau is a wonderful accompaniment that could easily be a meal on its own. This version with eggplant is particularly tasty and is great served with plain yogurt.

2 eggplant, cut into 1 in/2.5 cm cubes
salt
1/4 cup/60 mL olive oil
1 onion, sliced
14 oz/440 g canned tomatoes, drained and mashed
2 tablespoons chopped fresh parsley
1 tablespoon chopped fresh mint
3 cups/500 g long grain rice
3 cups/750 mL chicken stock

1 Sprinkle eggplant with salt and set aside for 30 minutes. Rinse under cold running water and pat dry with paper towels.

2 Heat oil in a large heavy-based skillet, add eggplant and cook, stirring frequently, for 5 minutes or until lightly browned. Remove eggplant from pan and set aside.

3 Add onion to pan and cook for 4-5 minutes or until soft. Stir in tomatoes, parsley, mint and reserved eggplant and cook, stirring frequently, for 5 minutes. Stir in rice and stock and bring to the boil. Reduce heat, cover and simmer for 30 minutes or until rice is tender. Allow to stand for 10 minutes before serving.

Serves 6

Lontong

Lontong are traditionally wrapped in young banana leaves. If these are not readily available, you can successfully substitute aluminum foil. The fried onion flakes used in the recipe can be purchased from Asian food stores.

young banana leaves or aluminum foil
vegetable oil
2 1/2 cups/500 g short grain rice, washed
2 tablespoons soy sauce
2 tablespoons fried onion flakes

1 If using banana leaves, drop them into boiling water to clean and soften. Remove leaves from water and pat dry with paper towels. Cut leaves or foil into 8 in/20 cm squares and brush lightly with oil.

2 Place a large spoonful of rice in the center of each square and fold over to completely enclose rice and make a neat parcel. When making the parcels, allow a little room for expansion during cooking. Tie each parcel with string to secure.

3 Bring a large saucepan of water to the boil, drop in rice bundles and simmer for 1 hour. To serve, drain bundles, unwrap and sprinkle with soy sauce and onion flakes.

Serves 6

Rose-scented Saffron Rice,
Pilau with Vegetables,
Lontong

Gingered Zucchini

2 tablespoons vegetable oil
2 teaspoons finely grated fresh ginger
1 onion, sliced
1 clove garlic, crushed
4 zucchini, cut into $^1/_2$ in/1 cm slices
$^1/_4$ cup/60 mL vegetable stock or water
freshly ground black pepper
1 tablespoon snipped fresh chives

1 Heat oil in a large skillet, add ginger, onion and garlic and stir-fry for 1-2 minutes. Add zucchini and stir-fry for 3-4 minutes longer.

2 Pour in stock or water and bring to the boil. Reduce heat and cook until zucchini are tender. Season to taste with black pepper, sprinkle with chives and serve immediately.

Serves 4

Carrots are also delicious cooked in this way, but remember that the cooking time will be a little longer.

Broccoli in Ginger Soy Sauce

1 tablespoon vegetable oil
1 large head broccoli, broken into florets
freshly ground black pepper

GINGER SOY SAUCE
1 tablespoon soy sauce
1 tablespoon grated fresh ginger
2 teaspoons cornstarch blended with $^1/_2$ cup/125 mL vegetable stock or water

1 Heat oil in a wok or skillet, add broccoli and stir-fry for 2-3 minutes or until broccoli changes color.

2 To make sauce, combine soy sauce, ginger and cornstarch mixture. Pour over broccoli in pan and cook, stirring, for 2-3 minutes or until sauce thickens. Season to taste with black pepper and serve immediately.

Serves 4

Fresh ginger freezes well. When you want to use it, simply grate the required amount off the piece of frozen ginger.

'It is said that ginger is a good remedy for, and can even help prevent, travel sickness.'

Broccoli in Ginger Soy Sauce, Pickled Ginger, Gingered Zucchini

Right: Mustard Potato Salad
Far right: Chili Beans and Bacon

Mustard Potato Salad

Mustard has been used as a condiment since at least Roman times. The Romans pounded the seeds and steeped them in wine. They also ate the leaves as a green vegetable. Mustard is frequently mentioned in the Bible and in Greek and Roman literature.

2 lb/1 kg tiny new potatoes, scrubbed

MUSTARD DRESSING

3 tablespoons dairy sour cream
3 tablespoons mayonnaise
2 tablespoons coarse grain mustard
2 tablespoons Dijon mustard

1 Boil or microwave potatoes until tender. Drain, refresh under cold running water, drain again and refrigerate until ready to serve.

2 To make dressing, place sour cream, mayonnaise, coarse grain and Dijon mustards in a bowl and mix to combine. Place potatoes in a salad bowl, spoon over dressing and serve.

Serves 6

Chili Beans and Bacon

1 tablespoon olive oil
1 teaspoon chili paste (sambal oelek)
1 onion, chopped
6 slices bacon, chopped
14 oz/440 g canned lima or butter beans, drained and rinsed
2 tablespoons chopped fresh parsley
freshly ground black pepper

1 Heat oil in a large skillet, add chili paste (sambal oelek), onion and bacon and cook, stirring constantly, for 4-5 minutes or until bacon is cooked.

2 Add beans and cook for 5 minutes longer or until heated through. Stir in parsley and season to taste with black pepper.

Serves 4

This easy vegetable dish can also be served as a main dish for two. Simply accompany with a tossed green salad and crusty bread rolls.

Below: Spinach Curry
Right: Spicy Wholewheat Parathas

Spinach Curry

This quick Spinach Curry makes a wonderful dish for a vegetarian meal or as an accompaniment to a mild meat dish.

1/4 cup/60 g ghee or clarified butter
1 onion, finely chopped
2 cloves garlic, crushed
2 small fresh red chilies, thinly sliced
1 teaspoon grated fresh ginger
1 bunch/1 lb/500 g spinach, stalks removed and leaves shredded
freshly ground black pepper

1 Melt ghee or butter in a skillet, add onion, garlic, chilies and ginger and stir-fry for 5 minutes or until onion is soft.

2 Add spinach leaves, toss to coat with spices and cook for 4-5 minutes or until spinach begins to wilt. Season to taste with black pepper and serve immediately.

Serves 4

Spicy Wholewheat Parathas

3 cups/375 g all-purpose flour
1 cup/155 g wholewheat all-purpose flour
$^{1}/_{2}$ cup/1 stick/125 g butter
$1^{1}/_{2}$ cups/375 mL water
8 oz/250 g mashed potato
1 cup/125 g shredded mature Cheddar cheese
2 teaspoons curry powder
1 teaspoon ground cumin

1 Place flour and wholewheat flour in a food processor and process to sift. Add $^{1}/_{4}$ cup/$^{1}/_{2}$ stick/60 g butter and process until mixture resembles coarse bread crumbs.

2 With machine running, add water and process to form a dough. Turn dough onto a lightly floured surface and knead for 5 minutes or until smooth. Set aside to stand for 5 minutes.

3 Place mashed potato, cheese, curry powder and cumin in a bowl and mix to combine.

4 Divide dough into twelve equal portions and press out each portion to form a 4 in/10 cm circle. Divide potato mixture between dough circles and spread evenly over dough, leaving a border around the edge. Fold dough circles in half to enclose the filling, then carefully roll again to form a 4 in/10 cm circle.

5 Melt remaining butter in a large skillet and cook a few parathas at a time for 3-4 minutes each side or until golden and cooked through.

Makes 12

Parathas are an unleavened Indian bread. This version with a cumin-flavored potato and cheese filling is delicious served with meat or vegetable curries.

Chili Onion Rings

1/2 cup/125 mL buttermilk or milk
2 fresh red chilies, seeded and chopped
2 large onions, cut into rings 1/4 in/5 mm thick
2 cups/250 g all-purpose flour
vegetable oil for deep-frying
2 tablespoons chili sauce or chutney

1 Place milk and chilies in a food processor or blender and process for 30 seconds. Transfer to a bowl, add onion rings and toss to coat with milk mixture.

2 Sift flour into a large bowl. Using a slotted spoon, remove onion rings from milk mixture, drain, add to bowl and coat onion rings in flour.

3 Heat oil in a large saucepan until a cube of bread dropped in browns in 50 seconds. Add a few onion rings at a time and cook for 2-3 minutes or until golden and crisp. Drain on paper towels and serve immediately with chili sauce or chutney.

Serves 4

To keep cooked onion rings warm, place on paper towels in an ovenproof dish in an oven set at 300°F/150°C.

Brussels Sprouts with Mustard

1 lb/500 g Brussels sprouts

MUSTARD SAUCE
1 tablespoon/15 g butter
1 tablespoon all-purpose flour
1/2 cup/125 mL hot milk
1 cup/250 mL chicken stock
2 teaspoons coarse grain mustard
1 tablespoon mayonnaise

1 Boil, steam or microwave Brussels sprouts until just tender. Drain, set aside and keep warm.

2 To make sauce, melt butter in a saucepan, add flour and cook, stirring, for 1 minute. Remove pan from heat and whisk in milk, then stock. Return pan to heat and cook, stirring, for 4-5 minutes or until sauce boils and thickens. Stir in mustard and mayonnaise. Spoon sauce over Brussels sprouts and serve immediately.

Serves 4

Try this Mustard Sauce poured over other vegetables such as cauliflower, broccoli or zucchini.

Brussels Sprouts with Mustard

Coriander Bean Salad

All parts of the coriander (cilantro) plant can be used. However you should be aware that if a recipe calls for fresh coriander you should not substitute it for the dried seeds or ground coriander (this is ground coriander seeds not leaf), as the two have completely different flavors.

1 lb/500 g shelled fresh lima beans or frozen lima beans
8 oz/250 g fresh or frozen sweet corn kernels
4 tomatoes, cut into wedges
6 spring onions, chopped
2 tablespoons chopped fresh coriander

CUMIN DRESSING
1/4 cup/60 mL olive oil
1/4 cup/60 mL lemon juice
1/2 teaspoon ground cumin
freshly ground black pepper

1 Boil, steam or microwave beans and sweet corn, separately, until tender. Place hot beans, sweet corn, tomatoes, spring onions and coriander in a bowl.

2 To make dressing, place oil, lemon juice, cumin and black pepper to taste in a screwtop jar and shake well to combine. Pour over bean mixture and toss to combine. Set aside, tossing occasionally, until beans are cool.

Serves 8

Ratatouille

Ratatouille is delicious as a filling for red or green peppers. These are great as the main course of a vegetarian meal.
To complete the meal, accompany the filled peppers with crusty French bread and a tossed green salad.

2 eggplant, cut into strips
salt
2 tablespoons olive oil
2 large red onions, sliced
2 cloves garlic, crushed
2 green peppers, sliced
14 oz/440 g canned tomatoes, undrained and mashed
1/3 cup/90 mL dry white wine
1 tablespoon chopped fresh oregano or 1 teaspoon dried oregano
1 tablespoon tomato paste
8 oz/250 g mushrooms, sliced
3 tablespoons chopped fresh parsley
freshly ground black pepper

1 Place eggplant in a colander set over a bowl and sprinkle with salt. Set aside to stand for 30 minutes, then rinse under cold running water and pat dry with paper towels.

2 Heat oil in a large skillet and cook onions, garlic and green peppers over a medium heat for 3-4 minutes or until onions are soft. Add eggplant, tomatoes, wine, oregano and tomato paste and cook, stirring, over a medium heat for 25-30 minutes or until mixture reduces and thickens. Stir in mushrooms and cook for 5 minutes longer. Add parsley and season to taste with black pepper. Serve hot, warm or at room temperature.

Serves 6

Coriander Bean Salad, Ratatouille

Pesto Potato Bake

Oven temperature
350°F, 180°C

The Pesto used in this recipe is also delicious tossed through pasta or boiled, steamed or microwaved vegetables such as squash or carrots.

8 potatoes, thickly sliced

PESTO
2 oz/60 g basil leaves
2 cloves garlic, crushed
2 tablespoons pine nuts (pignola)
$^{1}/_{2}$ cup/125 mL olive oil
4 tablespoons grated Parmesan cheese

SOUR CREAM TOPPING
$9^{1}/_{2}$ oz/300 g dairy sour cream
$^{1}/_{2}$ cup/60 g shredded mature Cheddar cheese
freshly ground black pepper

1 Boil, steam or microwave potato slices until almost tender. Drain, then layer in the base of a lightly greased baking dish.

2 To make Pesto, place basil, garlic, pine nuts (pignola), oil and Parmesan cheese in a food processor or blender and process until smooth. Spread over potatoes.

3 To make topping, spoon sour cream over Pesto and top with Cheddar and black pepper to taste. Bake for 10 minutes or until potatoes are tender and top is golden brown.

Serves 4

Pesto Potato Bake

Rosemary Sweet Potatoes

2 sweet potatoes, cut into thick slices
1 tablespoon finely chopped fresh rosemary
2 cloves garlic, crushed
1/4 cup/60 mL olive oil
freshly ground black pepper

Serves 4

1 Layer sweet potato slices in a lightly greased baking dish and sprinkle with rosemary.

2 Combine garlic and olive oil, drizzle over sweet potatoes and season to taste with black pepper. Bake for 30 minutes or until sweet potatoes are tender.

Oven temperature
350°F, 180°C

Tomato Basil Salad

2 large tomatoes, sliced
2 oz/60 g fresh basil leaves
1 red onion, sliced into rings

GARLIC DRESSING
2 cloves garlic, crushed
2 teaspoons olive oil
1 tablespoon lime or lemon juice
freshly ground black pepper

1 Cut each tomato slice in half and arrange alternately with basil leaves on a large serving platter. Place onion rings in center of platter.

2 To make dressing, place garlic, oil, lime or lemon juice and black pepper to taste in a screwtop jar and shake well to combine. Drizzle over salad.

Serves 4

Ever popular as an accompaniment to barbecued or broiled food, this salad adds color and flavor to any meal. Use fresh young basil leaves, or you might like to use mint leaves to create a Tomato Mint Salad – delicious with broiled or barbecued lamb chops.

Tomato Basil Salad

RECIPE COLLECTION

DESSERTS

For many people a meal without a dessert is incomplete. In this chapter you will find something to suit every taste and occasion – simple fruit desserts and hearty winter warmers for family meals and a selection of exciting recipes for those special occasions.

Lemon Pudding Cake

Lemon Pudding Cake

1 cup/7 oz superfine sugar
1/2 cup/1 stick/125 g butter, softened
1/2 cup/60 g self-rising flour, sifted
1 tablespoon finely grated lemon peel
1 tablespoon finely grated orange peel
2 tablespoons lemon juice
2 tablespoons orange juice
2 eggs, separated
1 cup/250 mL milk

1 Place sugar and butter in a bowl and beat until light and fluffy. Mix in flour, lemon and orange peel, lemon and orange juices.

2 Place egg yolks and milk in a small bowl and whisk to combine. Mix into citrus mixture.

3 Beat egg whites until stiff peaks form then fold into batter. Spoon into a greased 4 cup/1 liter capacity baking dish. Place dish in a baking pan with enough boiling water to come halfway up the sides of the dish. Bake for 45 minutes or until cooked. Serve hot with cream or ice cream if desired.

Serves 6

Oven temperature
350°F, 180°C

One of those magic puddings – as the pudding cooks it separates to give a layer of fluffy sponge over a tangy citrus sauce.

Whiskey Bread and Butter Pudding

6 peaches, peeled, pitted and sliced
3 tablespoons/45 g butter, softened
12 slices white bread, crusts removed
1 tablespoon ground cinnamon

CARAMEL
3/4 cup/185 g sugar
3/4 cup/185 mL water

WHISKEY CUSTARD
3 eggs
2/3 cup/4 1/2 oz superfine sugar
1 cup/250 mL milk, scalded
1 cup/250 mL cream, scalded
2 tablespoons whiskey

1 To make caramel, place sugar and water in a small saucepan and cook over a low heat, stirring, until sugar dissolves. Increase heat and simmer until caramel is a golden color. Pour caramel into base of a well-greased 10 in/25 cm round ovenproof dish and set aside.

2 Poach or microwave peaches until just tender. Drain well and set aside.

3 To make custard, place eggs and sugar in a bowl and whisk to combine. Whisk in milk, cream and whiskey.

4 Butter bread on one side, then cut into triangles. Place a layer of bread in base of prepared dish then top with a layer of peaches and sprinkle with cinnamon. Repeat layers, until bread, peaches and cinnamon are all used, ending with a bread layer. Carefully pour custard over the layers. Place dish in a large baking pan with enough hot water to come halfway up the sides of the dish and bake for 50-60 minutes or until custard is set. Stand for 15 minutes before turning out and serving.

Serves 8

Oven temperature
350°F, 180°C

Poured into the base of the baking dish, caramel adds a delicious flavor to this traditional English pudding. Baking it in a pan of hot water ensures a smooth, creamy custard.
If fresh peaches are unavailable drained canned peaches can be used instead – in which case there is no need to cook them.

Papaya and Cherry Salad

For something different you might like to use an orange liqueur such as Cointreau or Grand Marnier in place of the cherry brandy when making this salad.

2 large papaya, seeds removed
8 oz/250 g fresh cherries
2 tablespoons chopped fresh mint
3 tablespoons cherry brandy

Using a melon baller, scoop out papaya flesh. Place papaya balls, cherries, mint and cherry brandy in a bowl and toss to combine. Cover and refrigerate for 30 minutes before serving.

Serves 4

Right: Papaya and Cherry Salad
Far right: Berry Salad in Meringue Nests

Berry Salad in Meringue Nests

4 oz/125 g raspberries
4 oz/125 g blueberries or redcurrants
3 tablespoons Cointreau (orange liqueur)
14 oz/440 g canned apricot halves, drained and 3 tablespoons juice reserved

MERINGUE NESTS
3 egg whites
1/3 cup/75 g superfine sugar
1 teaspoon vanilla

1 To make nests, place egg whites in a bowl and beat until soft peaks form. Gradually add sugar, beating well after each addition, until mixture is thick and glossy. Beat in vanilla.

2 Draw 2 1/2 in/6 cm circles on a piece of nonstick parchment paper. Turn paper over and place on a lightly greased baking sheet. Place meringue mixture in a pastry bag fitted with a plain nozzle and, using circles as a guide, pipe meringue nests. Bake for 20 minutes, then reduce oven temperature to 250°F/120°C and bake for 25 minutes longer. Remove from oven and set aside to cool completely.

3 Place raspberries, blueberries or redcurrants and Cointreau (orange liqueur) in a bowl and toss to combine. Place apricot halves and reserved juice in a food processor or blender and process until smooth.

4 To serve, spoon 2 tablespoons apricot mixture on each serving plate, place a meringue nest in center of plate and fill with berry mixture. Serve immediately.

Serves 6

Oven temperature
300°F, 150°C

The Meringue Nests can be made ahead of time and will keep for up to a week if stored in an airtight container.

Passion Fruit Souffle

Oven temperature
350°F, 180°C

Individual soufflés are the perfect dessert after a rich or spicy main meal. While the actual mixing and cooking of the soufflés has to be left until just before serving, the Nectarine Cream and preparation of the dishes can be done in advance.

softened butter
superfine sugar
$^1/_2$ cup/125 g passion fruit pulp
$^2/_3$ cup/100 g confectioners' sugar
2 egg yolks
1 tablespoon orange juice
6 egg whites

NECTARINE CREAM

2 very ripe nectarines, peeled and pits removed
$1^1/_4$ cups/315 mL whipping cream
2 tablespoons confectioners' sugar
2 tablespoons Grand Marnier (orange liqueur)

1 Brush four $1^1/_2$ cup/375 mL capacity soufflé dishes with butter then sprinkle with superfine sugar. Turn dishes upside down to allow excess sugar to fall out.

2 Place passion fruit pulp, $^1/_2$ cup/$2^1/_2$ oz confectioners' sugar, egg yolks and orange juice in a large bowl and mix well to combine. Place egg whites in a mixing bowl and beat until soft peaks form, add remaining confectioners' sugar and beat until just combined. Mix one-quarter egg white mixture into the passion fruit mixture, then gently fold in the remaining egg whites. Spoon into prepared soufflé dishes and bake for 8-10 minutes or until well risen and golden.

3 To make Nectarine Cream, place nectarine flesh in a food processor or blender and process to purée. Place cream, confectioners' sugar and Grand Marnier in a bowl and beat until soft peaks form. Gently fold cream mixture into nectarine purée. Chill until ready to serve.

4 To serve, dust soufflés with confectioners' sugar and accompany with Nectarine Cream.

Serves 4

Passion Fruit Soufflé

Chocolate Log

$^{3}/_{4}$ cup/1$^{1}/_{2}$ sticks/185 g butter
$^{1}/_{4}$ cup/30 g cocoa powder
1 cup/250 mL hot water
6$^{1}/_{2}$ oz/200 g semi-sweet cooking chocolate, chopped
1 cup/220 g superfine sugar
$^{1}/_{2}$ cup/125 g ricotta cheese
$^{3}/_{4}$ cup/90 g all-purpose flour
1 cup/125 g self-rising flour
2 eggs

CHOCOLATE FILLING
200 g/6$^{1}/_{2}$ oz milk chocolate, melted
2 tablespoons whipping cream
$^{1}/_{2}$ cup/60 g chopped nuts

CHOCOLATE FROSTING
125 g/4 oz semi-sweet cooking chocolate
2 tablespoons/30 g butter

1 Place butter, cocoa powder, water, chocolate and sugar in a saucepan and cook over a medium heat, stirring constantly, until chocolate melts and ingredients are combined.

2 Transfer chocolate mixture to a large bowl. Beat in ricotta cheese, all-purpose flour, self-rising flour and eggs. Continue beating until mixture is smooth. Spoon mixture into a greased and parchment paper-lined 4$^{1}/_{2}$ x 8$^{1}/_{2}$ in /11 x 21 cm loaf pan and bake for 1$^{1}/_{2}$ hours or until cake is cooked when tested with a skewer. Allow cake to stand in pan for 5 minutes before turning onto a wire rack to cool completely.

3 To make filling, place chocolate, cream and nuts in a bowl and mix to combine. Cut cake horizontally into three layers. Spread two of the layers with filling, place one on top of the other, then top with the plain layer.

4 To make frosting, place chocolate and butter in top of a double boiler over simmering water and heat, stirring, until chocolate melts and mixture is smooth. Spread top and sides of cake with frosting and refrigerate until set.

Serves 10

Oven temperature
325°F, 160°C

For a special occasion this dessert is delicious served with whipped cream and fresh raspberries.

'In Italy ricotta can be made from cow's or sheep's milk. If made from sheep's milk it is known as ricotta pecora, *if from cow's milk* ricotta vaccina.'

Dark Chocolate Cake

Oven temperature
325°F, 160°C

3/4 cup/75 g cocoa powder
3/4 cup/185 mL boiling water
1 3/4 cups/220 g self-rising flour
1 1/2 cups/330 g superfine sugar
6 eggs, separated
1/4 cup/1/2 stick/60 g butter, melted

CREAM CHEESE FILLING
1 1/4 cups/200 g confectioners' sugar
1/4 cup/60 mL milk
1 teaspoon vanilla
2 tablespoons cocoa powder
8 oz/250 g cream cheese, softened

DECORATION
1 cup/125 g chopped nuts
4 oz/125 g milk chocolate
1 tablespoon butter
1 cup/250 mL whipping cream, whipped
1/2 cup/90 g whole hazelnuts (filberts)

1 Place cocoa powder in a small bowl. Gradually add boiling water to make a smooth paste. Place flour and sugar in a large bowl, add cocoa mixture, egg yolks and butter and beat until smooth.

2 Place egg whites in a large bowl and beat until soft peaks form. Fold egg white mixture into cocoa mixture. Spoon batter into a greased and parchment paper-lined 9 in/23 cm springform pan and bake for 1 hour or until cake is cooked when tested with a skewer. Cool in pan for 5 minutes then turn onto a wire rack to cool completely.

3 To make filling, place confectioners' sugar, milk, vanilla and cocoa powder in a bowl and mix to make a smooth paste. Place cream cheese and cocoa mixture in a food processor or blender and process until smooth. Remove 1/2 cup of filling and set aside – this is used for the sides of the cake.

4 Cut cake horizontally into three layers. Spread two of the layers with filling, place one on top of the other, then top with the plain layer. Spread reserved filling around sides of cake. Chill cake for 1 hour or until filling is set.

5 To decorate the cake, place chopped nuts on a piece of waxed paper and roll cake in nuts to coat sides. Place milk chocolate and butter in top of double boiler over simmering water and heat, stirring, until chocolate melts and mixture is smooth. Spread top of cake with chocolate mixture and refrigerate until set. Just prior to serving, pipe rosettes of whipped cream around edge of cake and place a whole hazelnut (filbert) in the middle of each rosette.

Serves 10

This rich chocolate cake makes the ideal adult birthday cake.

Dark Chocolate Cake

Sabayon with Berries

3 egg yolks
$^1/_4$ cup/60 g/2 oz superfine sugar
2 tablespoons Cointreau (orange liqueur)
1 teaspoon plain gelatin
$^1/_4$ cup/60 mL white wine
$^1/_2$ cup/125 mL whipping cream, lightly whipped
8 oz/250 g fresh berries of your choice

Serves 4

1 Place egg yolks, sugar and Cointreau in top of a double boiler and place over boiling water. Cook, whisking mixture constantly, for 3 minutes or until thick. Remove pan from heat and set aside.

2 Place gelatin and wine in a small bowl and dissolve over a saucepan of simmering water. Whisk gelatin mixture into egg mixture and continue to whisk until mixture is cool.

3 Fold cream into egg yolk mixture, spoon into individual serving glasses and chill. Serve with berries.

Sweet sabayon is the French version of the Italian dessert zabaglione. In this recipe the basic sabayon sauce is set with gelatin to make a delectable summer dessert.

Sabayon with Berries

Passion Fruit Pavlova

Passion Fruit Pavlova

6 egg whites
1 cup/220 g superfine sugar
$^{1}/_{4}$ teaspoon cream of tartar
2 teaspoons cornstarch
$1^{1}/_{2}$ cups/375 mL whipping cream, whipped
pulp of 4 passion fruit
fresh mint leaves, cut into fine strips

Serves 8

1 Place egg whites in a large mixing bowl and beat until soft peaks form. Gradually add sugar, beating well after each addition until mixture is thick and glossy.

2 Fold cream of tartar and cornstarch into egg white mixture.

3 Grease and line the base and sides of a 9 in/23 cm springform pan with nonstick parchment paper, then lightly dust with extra cornstarch. Spoon meringue into pan and spread out evenly. Bake for $1^{1}/_{2}$ hours, then turn off oven and allow pavlova to cool for 30 minutes with oven door ajar. Remove pavlova from oven and set aside to cool completely.

4 Top cold pavlova with cream and decorate with passion fruit pulp and mint strips.

Oven temperature
250°F, 120°C

Both Australia and New Zealand claim to have created this truly marvelous dessert. However, both agree that it is named after the famous Russian ballerina, Anna Pavlova.

Mixed Fruit Brulee

For this dessert choose fruit in season. In winter a combination of apples, bananas and oranges with dried apricots soaked in brandy makes a delicious alternative.

1 large papaya, seeds removed, peeled and flesh cut into 3/4 in/2 cm cubes
4 kiwifruit, peeled and cut into 3/4 in/2 cm cubes
4 oz/125 g strawberries
1 cup/250 mL whipping cream, whipped

CARAMEL TOPPING
3 tablespoons water
1 cup/220 g superfine sugar

1 To make topping, place water and sugar in a heavy-based saucepan and cook over a medium heat, stirring until sugar dissolves. Bring mixture to the boil and boil without stirring until sugar syrup is a golden brown. Swirl pan once or twice during cooking.

2 Arrange papaya, kiwifruit and strawberries on individual serving plates, top with cream and spoon over topping. Serve immediately.

Serves 4

Left: *Mixed Fruit Brûlée*
Below: *Chocolate Tiramisu*

Chocolate Tiramisu

2 eggs, separated
1/2 cup/100 g superfine sugar
1 1/2 cups/375 g mascarpone
1/4 cup/60 mL brandy
6 1/2 oz/200 g sponge ladyfingers
1/4 cup/60 mL very strong black coffee
1/4 cup/30 g cocoa powder, sifted

1 Place egg yolks and sugar in a bowl and beat until light and fluffy. Add mascarpone and brandy and beat until mixture is smooth.

2 Place egg whites in a clean bowl and beat until soft peaks form. Carefully fold egg white mixture into egg yolk mixture.

3 Place half the ladyfingers in the base of a large serving bowl, sprinkle with half the coffee and top with half the mascarpone mixture. Repeat layers and dust top of dessert with cocoa powder. Chill until served.

Serves 8

Mascarpone is a fresh cheese made from cream. It is unsalted, buttery and rich with a fat content of 90 per cent and mostly is used as a dessert, either alone or as an ingredient.
Mascarpone is available from delicatessens and some supermarkets. If it is unavailable, mix one part sour cream to three parts lightly whipped whipping cream and use in its place.

Miniature Paris Brest

Oven temperature
425°F, 220°C

CHOUX PASTRY
1 cup/250 mL water
5 tablespoons/75 g butter, cut into small pieces
3/4 cup/90 g all-purpose flour, sifted
3 eggs

FILLING
3/4 cup/185 mL whipping cream, whipped
8 oz/250 g diced fresh fruit

TOFFEE
1 cup/250 g sugar
1/3 cup/90 mL water

1 To make pastry, place water and butter in a saucepan and slowly bring to the boil. As soon as the mixture boils, quickly stir in flour, using a wooden spoon. Cook over a low heat, stirring constantly, for 2 minutes or until mixture is smooth and leaves sides of pan. Remove from heat and set aside to cool slightly. Beat in eggs one at a time, beating well after each addition until mixture is light and glossy.

2 Line baking sheets with nonstick parchment paper and trace 2 in/5 cm circles on it. Spoon pastry mixture into a pastry bag fitted with a 1/2 in/1 cm plain nozzle. Turn paper over and pipe two rows of pastry, one on top of the other, inside the traced circles. Bake for 8 minutes. Prop oven door open using the handle of a wooden spoon and cook pastries for 10 minutes longer, or until golden and crisp. Remove from sheet and cool on a wire rack. Split pastries in half using a serrated knife. Return to the oven and bake at 250°F/120°C for 5 minutes or until pastries dry out. Set aside to cool completely.

3 Fill bottom halves of pastries with whipped cream and top with fruit. Replace lids and set aside.

4 To make toffee, place sugar and water in a small saucepan. Cook over a medium heat, stirring constantly until sugar dissolves. Continue to cook without stirring until mixture is golden. Remove from heat and stand until bubbles subside. Spin toffee and decorate pastries. Serve within an hour.

Makes 18

To spin toffee, coat the back of two wooden spoons with the toffee, place them back to back and gently pull apart. As a thread of toffee is formed continue bringing spoons together and pulling apart until the toffee starts to set and threads are formed. Repeat to use all the toffee.

Choux pastry is easy to make. Just remember not to tip the flour in before the water mixture is boiling and do not add all the eggs at once.

Miniature Paris Brest

Citrus Meringue Pie

Easy Mango Ice Cream

3 mangoes, peeled, seeded and chopped
2 tablespoons lemon juice
$^{3}/_{4}$ cup/170 g superfine sugar
2 eggs, separated
1 cup/250 mL whipping cream

1 Place mango flesh, lemon juice and sugar in a food processor or blender and process until smooth. Transfer mango mixture to a bowl and refrigerate.

2 Place egg whites in a bowl, beat until stiff peaks form and set aside. Place egg yolks in a separate bowl, beat until thick and creamy and set aside. Place cream in another bowl and whip until soft peaks form. Gently fold whipped cream into egg yolk mixture, then fold in egg whites. Finally, fold the egg mixture into the mango mixture. Spoon into a freezerproof container and freeze until solid.

Serves 4

If you have an ice cream maker, make the ice cream as described in the recipe and freeze in the ice cream maker, following the manufacturer's instructions.

Citrus Meringue Pie

SHORT PASTRY
2 1/2 cups/315 g all-purpose flour
1 teaspoon superfine sugar
3/4 cup/1 1/2 sticks/185 g unsalted (sweet) butter, chilled and cut into small squares
1/4-1/2 cup/60-125 mL iced water

CITRUS FILLING
5 egg yolks
1 1/2 cups/375 mL sweetened condensed milk
1/4 cup/60 mL lemon juice
2 tablespoons lime juice
2 tablespoons orange juice
1 egg white

MERINGUE TOPPING
5 egg whites
1/4 teaspoon cream of tartar
3/4 cup/170 g superfine sugar

1 To make pastry, place flour, sugar and butter in a food processor and process until mixture resembles fine bread crumbs. With machine running, slowly add iced water until a firm dough forms. Turn dough onto a lightly floured surface and knead until smooth. Wrap dough in plastic wrap and refrigerate for 30 minutes.

2 Roll out dough to fit an 8 in/20 cm pie dish. Line pastry shell with nonstick parchment paper, weigh down with uncooked rice and bake for 10-15 minutes. Remove rice and paper, and cook pastry shell for 5-10 minutes longer or until pastry is golden. Set aside to cool.

3 To make filling, place egg yolks, condensed milk, lemon juice, lime juice and orange juice in a bowl and mix to combine. Place egg white in a small bowl and beat until stiff peaks form. Fold egg white into egg yolk mixture and spoon into pastry shell.

4 To make topping, place egg whites and cream of tartar in a large bowl and beat until frothy. Gradually add sugar, beating well after each addition. Continue beating until stiff peaks form and the mixture is glossy. Cover filling with meringue, sealing to edge of pastry. Reduce oven temperature to 300°F/150°C. Bake for 10 minutes or until topping is golden.

Serves 6

Oven temperature
400°F, 200°C

For best results when making meringue, beat the egg whites until frothy then slowly beat in the sugar. The secret to a really good meringue is to have as much sugar as possible dissolved on completion of beating.

Easy Mango Ice Cream

Beef wrapped in Pastry

Oven temperature
425°F, 220°C

Succulent beef surrounded by mushrooms and wrapped in puff pastry, is a dish that is sure to impress. With these step-by-step instructions you can see just how easy it is to make.

1/4 cup/1/2 stick/60 g butter
2 lb/1 kg rib eye (Delmonico) roast, in one piece, trimmed of all visible fat
1 onion, chopped
12 oz/375 g button mushrooms, finely chopped
freshly ground black pepper
pinch ground nutmeg
1 tablespoon chopped fresh parsley
2 sheets prerolled frozen puff pastry, thawed
1 egg, lightly beaten

RED WINE SAUCE

1 cup/250 mL red wine
1 teaspoon finely chopped fresh thyme or 1/4 teaspoon dried thyme
1 teaspoon finely chopped fresh parsley
1/3 cup/90 g butter, cut into small pieces
2 teaspoons cornstarch blended with 1 tablespoon water

1 Melt half the butter in a large skillet. When sizzling, add beef and cook over a medium heat for 10 minutes, turning to brown and seal all sides. Remove meat from pan and set aside to cool completely.

2 Melt remaining butter in skillet and cook onion for 5 minutes or until soft. Add mushrooms and cook, stirring, for 15 minutes or until mushrooms give up all their juices and these have evaporated. Season to taste with black pepper and nutmeg, stir in parsley and set aside to cool completely.

3 If necessary roll out one sheet of pastry to a length 4 in/10 cm longer than beef and wide enough to wrap around beef. Spread half the mushroom mixture down center of pastry and place beef on top. Spread remaining mushroom mixture on top of beef. Cut out corners of pastry.

Brush pastry edges with egg. Wrap pastry around beef like a parcel, tucking in ends. Place pastry-wrapped beef seam side down on a lightly greased baking sheet and freeze for 10 minutes.

4 Roll out remaining pastry sheet to a 12 in /30 cm square and cut into strips 1/2 in/1 cm wide. Remove beef from freezer and brush pastry all over with egg. Arrange 5 pastry strips diagonally over pastry parcel, then arrange remaining 5 more strips diagonally in opposite direction. Brush top of strips only with egg and bake for 30 minutes for medium-rare beef. Place on a warmed serving platter and set aside to rest in a warm place for 10 minutes.

5 To make sauce, place wine in a small saucepan and cook over a medium heat until reduced by half. Add thyme, parsley and black pepper to taste. Remove pan from heat and quickly whisk in one piece of butter at a time, ensuring that each piece is completely whisked in and melted before adding the next. Whisk in cornstarch mixture and cook over a medium heat, stirring until sauce thickens. Serve with sliced beef.

Serves 6

Beef wrapped in Pastry

Egg Rolls

Wonton or egg roll wrappers are available from Asian food stores and some supermarkets.

8 oz/250 g pork tenderloin
1 tablespoon vegetable oil
1 red pepper, cut into strips
4 spring onions, chopped
$3^1/2$ oz/100 g bean sprouts
6 lettuce leaves, shredded
2 teaspoons cornstarch blended with
1 tablespoon water
1 tablespoon soy sauce
20 wonton or egg roll wrappers
oil for deep-frying

1 Slice pork thinly and cut crosswise into narrow strips.

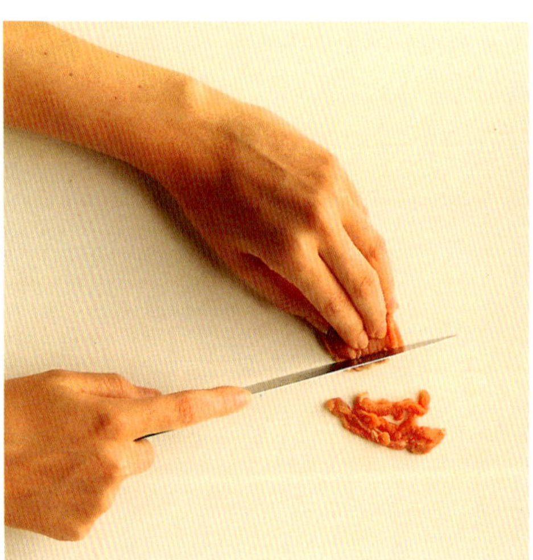

2 Heat vegetable oil in a skillet and stir-fry pork for 2-3 minutes or until it changes color.

3 Add red pepper and spring onions to pan and stir-fry for 3 minutes. Stir in bean sprouts, lettuce and cornstarch mixture, bring to the boil and cook, stirring, until mixture thickens. Stir in soy sauce and remove pan from heat and set aside to cool completely.

4 Place 2 tablespoons filling in the center of each wonton wrapper, fold one corner over the filling, then tuck in the sides and roll up, sealing with water.

5 Heat oil in a large saucepan until a cube of bread browns in 50 seconds and cook a few Egg Rolls at a time for 3-4 minutes or until golden. Drain on paper towels and serve immediately.

Makes 20

These Egg Rolls are also delicious made with beef, chicken or shrimp in place of the pork.

Egg Rolls

Italian Meatballs with Egg Sauce

When shaping ground meat, dampen your hands and work on a lightly floured or dampened surface – this will prevent the meat from sticking to your hands and the surface. An egg added to meat mixtures binds them and makes them easier to shape.

$^1/_2$ cup/30 g fresh bread crumbs
$^1/_2$ cup/125 mL milk
1 lb/500 g lean ground lamb
1 onion, finely chopped
pinch ground cloves
$^1/_2$ teaspoon ground cinnamon
1 egg
$^1/_3$ cup/60 g currants
$^1/_2$ cup/60 g toasted pine nuts (pignola)
3 cups/750 mL chicken stock

EGG SAUCE
3 eggs
2 tablespoons water
3 tablespoons lemon juice
freshly ground black pepper

1 Place bread crumbs in a bowl, pour milk over and set aside to soak for 5 minutes. Place lamb in a large bowl, add bread crumb mixture, onion, cloves, cinnamon, egg, currants and pine nuts (pignola), and mix to combine. Using wet hands roll mixture into small balls. Place meatballs on a plate lined with plastic wrap and refrigerate for 15 minutes.

2 Place stock in a large skillet and bring to the boil over a medium heat. Place meatballs in stock, bring back to the boil, then reduce heat and simmer for 30 minutes, turning meatballs occasionally. Using a slotted spoon, remove meatballs from stock and place on a warmed serving dish. Set aside and keep warm. Reserve 3 tablespoons stock to use in sauce.

3 To make sauce, place eggs, water and lemon juice in a saucepan and whisk to combine. Whisk in reserved hot stock and cook over a low heat, stirring constantly and without boiling for 3-4 minutes or until sauce thickens. Season to taste with black pepper and spoon over meatballs. Serve immediately.

Serves 4

For a quick version of this dish you can cook the meatballs in the microwave. When cooking in the microwave there is no need to use stock, simply place the meatballs in a round microwave-safe dish, cover with a lid or plastic wrap and cook on HIGH (100%) for 7-10 minutes or until meatballs are cooked. Rearrange the meatballs after 5 minutes of cooking, placing the center ones on the outside and the outside ones in the center. Make the sauce as described above while the meatballs are cooking, using 3 tablespoons of vegetable cooking water in place of the stock.

Italian Meatballs with Egg Sauce

English Pork Pies

Oven temperature
400°F, 200°C

4 cups/500 g all-purpose flour, sifted
1 tablespoon baking powder
8 oz/250 g lard, chopped
approximately $1\frac{1}{2}$ cups/375 mL boiling water
1 egg, lightly beaten

PORK FILLING

1 lb/500 g lean ground pork tenderloin
1 cup/60 g fresh bread crumbs
1 small onion, grated
$\frac{1}{2}$ teaspoon ground coriander
$\frac{1}{4}$ teaspoon ground nutmeg
$\frac{1}{2}$ teaspoon dried thyme
$\frac{1}{4}$ teaspoon ground sage
1 egg, lightly beaten
2 tablespoons milk

1 To make filling, place pork, bread crumbs, onion, coriander, nutmeg, thyme, sage, egg and milk in a bowl and mix to combine.

2 Place flour, baking powder and lard in a food processor and process until mixture resembles fine bread crumbs. With machine running, slowly add boiling water to form a stiff dough. Transfer pastry to a bowl, cover and set aside to rest for 30 minutes.

3 Divide pastry into two portions, one portion two-thirds larger than the other. Roll out the larger portion to $\frac{1}{8}$ in/3 mm thick and using a saucer as a guide cut out six 6 in/15 cm circles. Use pastry circles to line six individual soufflé or custard cups. Spoon in filling.

4 Roll out remaining pastry to $\frac{1}{8}$ in/3 mm thick and cut out six 3 in/7.5 cm circles. Brush rim of each pastry shell with a little water and top with pastry circles.

5 Crimp edges of pastry to seal, cut steam vents in tops, brush with beaten egg and bake for 40 minutes or until golden brown.

Makes 6

Traditionally served cold, pork pies are a substantial addition to a packed lunch or a delicious picnic treat. For a casual weekend lunch, you might like to serve a pork pie as part of a Ploughman's Lunch with a selection of cheese, chutneys and wholewheat rolls.

English Pork Pies

Roast Beef with Yorkshire Puddings

Oven temperature
375°F, 190°C

This time plan will ensure that you get your roast dinner cooked and on the table without any fuss.

2 hours before serving
(Note: 2 hours for medium beef or $1^3/4$ hours before serving for rare beef)
Place meat on to cook for 30 minutes.
Make Horseradish Cream, cover and refrigerate until just prior to serving.

After 30 minutes of cooking
Add carrots, onions and parsnips to meat dish.

1 hour before serving
Place potatoes on to cook.
Prepare a green vegetable of your choice, cover and refrigerate until ready to cook.

After 1 hour of cooking
Increase oven temperature to 425°F/220°C and cook beef for 15 minutes longer for rare beef and 30 minutes longer for medium beef.

20 minutes before serving
Prepare Yorkshire Puddings.

15 minutes before serving
Cook Yorkshire Puddings.
Make gravy and boil, steam or microwave prepared green vegetable.

4 lb/2 kg standing rib roast of beef
2 tablespoons vegetable oil
freshly ground black pepper
6 potatoes, halved
3 carrots, halved
6 onions, peeled
3 parsnips, halved
$^2/_3$ cup/170 mL beef stock

YORKSHIRE PUDDINGS
$^3/_4$ cup/90 g all-purpose flour
1 egg, lightly beaten
$^1/_3$ cup/90 mL milk
$^1/_4$ cup/60 mL water
3 tablespoons/45 g beef dripping

HORSERADISH CREAM
$^1/_2$ cup/125 mL whipping cream
1 tablespoon bottled horseradish

1 Place beef in a roasting pan, fat side up. Brush with 1 tablespoon oil, season to taste with black pepper and bake for 30 minutes.

2 Brush a baking dish with oil and heat in the oven. Add potatoes and bake for 1 hour or until potatoes are tender, turning halfway through cooking. Place carrots, onions and parsnips around beef and cook for 15 minutes then turn vegetables over and cook for 15 minutes longer. Increase oven temperature to 425°F/220°C and bake for 15 minutes longer for rare beef or 30 minutes longer for medium beef. Allow meat to rest in a warm place for 10-15 minutes before carving. Reserve roasting pan and cooking juices.

3 To make Yorkshire Puddings, sift flour into a bowl and season to taste with black pepper. Place egg, milk and water in a bowl and whisk to combine. Make a well in the center of the flour mixture, pour in egg mixture and beat slowly to incorporate wet ingredients. Place 1 teaspoon beef dripping in each of six muffin cups and heat in oven until dripping is sizzling. Divide pudding batter between muffin cups and cook at 425°F/220°C for 10-15 minutes.

4 Skim fat off pan juices in roasting pan. Place pan on top of the stove and cook over a low heat, stirring to scrape up caramelized juices. Stir in stock, bring to simmering and simmer for 10 minutes or until sauce reduces and thickens. Pour into a gravy boat and set aside to keep warm.

5 To make Horseradish Cream, whip cream until soft peaks form. Fold in horseradish and season to taste with black pepper.

Serves 6

Roast Beef with Yorkshire Puddings

Chicken with Spinach Filling

Oven temperature
350°F, 180°C

4 chicken marylands (uncut leg and thigh joints)
2 tablespoons/30 g butter, melted

SPINACH FILLING
4 oz/125 g frozen spinach, thawed
1 clove garlic, crushed
1/2 cup/125 g ricotta or cottage cheese, drained
2 teaspoons grated Parmesan cheese
1 teaspoon finely grated lemon peel
pinch ground nutmeg

TOMATO SAUCE
10 oz/310 g canned tomato purée
2 teaspoons Worcestershire sauce

Chicken with Spinach Filling

1 To make filling, squeeze spinach to remove excess liquid. Place spinach, garlic, ricotta or cottage cheese, Parmesan cheese, lemon peel and nutmeg in a bowl and mix to combine.

2 Using your fingers, loosen skin on chicken, starting at thigh end.

3 Push filling gently under skin down into the drumstick. Arrange chicken pieces in a baking dish, brush with melted butter and bake for 35-40 minutes.

4 To make sauce, place tomato purée and Worcestershire sauce in a saucepan, bring to simmering and simmer for 3-4 minutes. Serve sauce with chicken.

Serves 4

Drumsticks can be used in place of the chicken marylands if you wish.

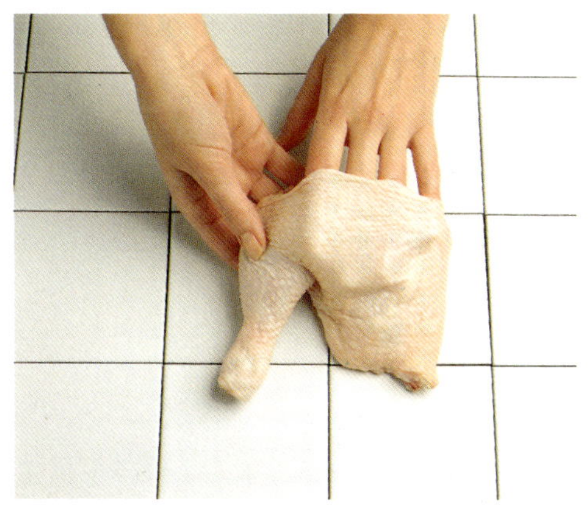

Frozen chicken should be completely thawed before cooking. Thaw birds in refrigerator for 24-36 hours or in microwave on DEFROST (30%) for 10-15 minutes per 1 lb/500 g of chicken. Rinse cavity of chicken under cold running water to ensure that there are no remaining ice crystals.

Spicy Chicken Pies

Oven temperature
375°F, 190°C

PASTRY
3 cups/375 g all-purpose flour
1/3 cup/90 g butter, cut into pieces
1/3 cup/90 g lard, cut into pieces
1/3 cup/90 mL cold water
1 egg, beaten

SPICY CHICKEN FILLING
2 tablespoons/30 g butter
2 oz/60 g button mushrooms, chopped
1 onion, chopped
2 teaspoons garam masala
1/4 cup/30 g all-purpose flour
3/4 cup/185 mL chicken stock
10 oz/315 g cooked chicken, diced
1/4 cup/60 g sweet corn kernels
freshly ground black pepper

1 To make filling, melt butter in a saucepan and cook mushrooms, onion and garam masala over a medium heat for 3-4 minutes or until onion is soft. Stir in flour and cook for 1 minute longer. Add stock and bring to the boil, stirring constantly. Reduce heat and simmer, stirring, for 2 minutes. Remove pan from heat, stir in chicken and sweet corn, season to taste with black pepper and set aside to cool completely.

Spicy Chicken Pies

2 To make pastry, place flour, butter and lard in a food processor and process until mixture resembles fine bread crumbs. With machine running, add water and process to form a firm dough. Turn dough onto a lightly floured surface and knead until smooth.

3 Take two-thirds of the dough and cut into four portions. Roll out each portion to fit a 5 in/12.5 cm loose-based, fluted tart pan. Line tart pans with pastry, press pastry into flutes, but do not trim top edge. Cut remaining pastry into four portions and roll out each portion to make a lid for each pie.

4 Spoon cold filling into tart shells. Dampen edges of pastry in pans and cover with pastry lids. Using a flat-bladed knife, press edges together to seal and cut off excess pastry. Gather together pastry trimmings, re-roll, then cut out pastry leaves and use to decorate tops of pies. Brush tops with beaten egg.

5 Place pies on a baking sheet and bake for 40-45 minutes or until pastry is golden. Remove pies from oven and set aside to cool. When cool, remove from tart pans.

Serves 4

These pies are a delicious picnic food served with a fruit chutney and a crisp salad.

'Delicious as picnic fare or in a packed lunch, you will want to keep a supply of these pies in your freezer.'

Perfect Roast Turkey

Oven temperature
350°F, 180°C

8 lb/4 kg turkey
1/4 cup/1/2 stick/60 g butter, melted
1 cup/250 mL chicken stock

VEAL FORCEMEAT
2 tablespoons/30 g butter
1 onion, finely chopped
1 slice bacon, finely chopped
8 oz/250 g lean ground veal
3 cups/185 g fresh bread crumbs
1/2 teaspoon finely grated lemon peel
1/2 teaspoon finely chopped fresh parsley
1/2 teaspoon dried sage
pinch ground nutmeg
1 egg, lightly beaten
freshly ground black pepper

CHESTNUT STUFFING
14 oz/440 g canned chestnut purée, sieved
2 cooking apples, cored, peeled and shredded
3 cups/185 g fresh bread crumbs
1 onion, finely chopped
1 stalk celery, finely chopped
4 tablespoons finely chopped walnuts
1 tablespoon finely chopped fresh parsley
3 tablespoons/45 g butter, melted
1 egg, lightly beaten
pinch ground nutmeg
freshly ground black pepper

Perfect Roast Turkey

1 To make forcemeat, melt butter in a skillet and cook onion and bacon for 4-5 minutes or until bacon is crisp. Add ground veal, bread crumbs, lemon peel, parsley, sage, nutmeg, egg and black pepper to taste. Mix well to combine.

2 To make stuffing, place chestnut purée, apples, bread crumbs, onion, celery, walnuts, parsley, butter, egg, nutmeg and black pepper to taste in a bowl and mix to combine.

3 Remove giblets and neck from turkey. Wipe turkey inside and out and dry well. Place stuffing in body cavity and lightly fill neck end of turkey with forcemeat. Secure openings with metal or bamboo skewers. Tuck wings under body of turkey and tie legs together.

4 Place turkey on a rack in a roasting pan. Brush with butter, then pour chicken stock into pan. Bake for 3-3$^{1}/_{2}$ hours or until tender. Baste frequently with pan juices during cooking. Set aside in a warm place to stand for 20 minutes before carving.

Serves 10

It is safest to defrost a frozen turkey in the refrigerator for 36-48 hours. Actual defrosting time will of course depend on the size of the bird. Once defrosted, wash bird and rinse out cavity, then pat dry using paper towels. Make sure that there are no ice crystals left in the cavity.

'Cooks have developed many wonderful turkey dishes for special occasions with delicious stuffings and accompaniments. Try this Roast Turkey for a Christmas or Thanksgiving dinner.'

Crusty Chicken Goulash

Oven temperature
350°F, 180°C

2 tablespoons vegetable oil
2 large onions, chopped
$1^1/2$ tablespoons paprika
2 tablespoons seasoned all-purpose flour
1 lb/500 g boned, skinned chicken breast halves, cut into strips
1 tablespoon tomato paste
$^1/2$ cup/125 mL red wine
$^1/2$ cup/125 mL chicken stock
3 tablespoons plain yogurt

SOUR CREAM CRUST
$^1/2$ cup/1 stick/125 g butter, softened
$1^1/4$ cups/300 g dairy sour cream
1 egg
1 cup/125 g self-rising flour, sifted
1 tablespoon chopped fresh parsley

Crusty Chicken Goulash

1 Heat 1 tablespoon oil in a large skillet and cook onions, stirring, over a medium heat for 5-6 minutes or until golden. Remove onions from pan and set aside. Combine paprika and flour in a plastic bag, add chicken, shake to coat with flour mixture, then shake off excess flour mixture.

2 Heat remaining oil in skillet and cook chicken, stirring, over a medium heat for 2-3 minutes. Return onions to pan, stir in tomato paste, wine and stock. Bring to the boil, stirring constantly, then reduce heat, cover and simmer for 6-7 minutes. Remove pan from heat, stir in yogurt and set aside to cool.

3 To make crust, place butter, sour cream and egg in a bowl. Stir in flour and parsley and mix well to combine.

4 To assemble, place crust mixture in an 8 cup/2 liter lightly greased ovenproof dish and work mixture to cover sides and base of dish.

5 Spoon filling into crust, cover with lid of dish and bake for 35 minutes. Remove lid and bake for 10 minutes longer.

Serves 4

Serve this delicious chicken with a tossed green salad or a boiled, steamed or microwaved green vegetable such as green beans, zucchini, snow peas or asparagus.

'A chicken goulash surrounded by a rich sour cream crust is just the thing for that special occasion.'

Cheesy Mushroom Strata

Oven temperature
350°F, 180°C

1/4 cup/1/2 stick/60 g butter
3 slices bacon, chopped
14 oz/440 g mushrooms, sliced
4 spring onions, chopped
1 small green pepper, chopped
1 small red pepper, chopped
6 thick slices white bread, crusts removed
1 cup/125 g shredded mature Cheddar cheese
6 eggs
2 cups/500 mL milk
1 tablespoon mayonnaise
1 teaspoon Dijon mustard
1 teaspoon Worcestershire sauce
2 tablespoons chopped fresh parsley

1 Melt butter in a large skillet, add bacon and cook for 4-5 minutes or until crisp. Stir in mushrooms, spring onions and green and red peppers and cook for 5 minutes longer or until mushrooms are soft.

2 Cut bread slices into 1 in/2.5 cm pieces. Place half the bread in the base of a lightly greased 7 x 11 in/18 x 28 cm ovenproof dish. Spoon mushroom mixture over and top with remaining bread. Sprinkle with cheese.

3 Place eggs, milk, mayonnaise, mustard and Worcestershire sauce in a bowl and whisk to combine. Carefully pour egg mixture over bread mixture and sprinkle with parsley. Bake for 50-60 minutes or until firm.

Serves 6

This recipe is an ideal one to cook ahead. Prepare the whole dish, and refrigerate overnight. Bake when you are ready the next day. The flavor develops if you allow the strata to stand before cooking.

Cheesy Mushroom Strata

Cheese Sticks and Braids

Oven temperature
400°F, 200°C

1 cup/125 g all-purpose flour
$^{1}/_{2}$ teaspoon baking powder
$^{1}/_{4}$ teaspoon salt
$^{1}/_{4}$ teaspoon cayenne pepper or to taste
$^{1}/_{4}$ teaspoon dry mustard
$^{3}/_{4}$ cup/90 g grated Parmesan cheese
$^{1}/_{3}$ cup/90 g butter
3 egg yolks
2 teaspoons cold water
1 egg white, lightly beaten
paprika

The sticks look attractive served in a pastry ring. To make a pastry ring, cut a circle using a $2^{1}/_{2}$ in/6 cm round cutter, then cut out the center to form a ring using a $1^{3}/_{4}$ in/4.5 cm round cutter. Bake as for sticks and braids.

1 Place flour, baking powder, salt, cayenne pepper and mustard in a food processor and process to sift. Reserve 3 teaspoons Parmesan cheese and set aside. Add butter and remaining Parmesan cheese to flour mixture and process until mixture resembles fine bread crumbs. With machine running, slowly add egg yolks and water to form a dough.

2 Turn dough onto a lightly floured surface and knead briefly. Roll out dough to a rectangle 9 x 12 in/23 x 30 cm. Trim edges and brush dough with egg white, then sprinkle with reserved Parmesan cheese. Cut dough in half lengthwise, then into $^{1}/_{4}$ in/5 mm strips crosswise. To make braids, twist two strips together.

3 Place sticks or braids on lightly greased baking sheets and bake for 8-10 minutes or until sticks or braids are lightly browned. Allow to cool on sheets for 2-3 minutes before transferring to a wire rack to cool completely. When cold, dust sticks or braids with paprika.

Makes 100 sticks or 50 braids

CRUNCHY CAMEMBERT

3 x 4 oz/125 g wheels Camembert cheese
2 teaspoons all-purpose flour
$^1/_2$ teaspoon dry mustard
$^1/_2$ teaspoon dried mixed herbs
freshly ground black pepper
$^1/_4$ cup/30 g dry bread crumbs
$^1/_2$ teaspoon chili powder or to taste
1 egg, beaten
vegetable oil for deep-frying

BLUEBERRY SAUCE
2 teaspoons cornstarch
$^1/_3$ cup/90 mL water
8 oz/250 g fresh or frozen blueberries
$^1/_4$ cup/60 g sugar
$^1/_4$ teaspoon ground nutmeg
2 teaspoons lemon juice

1 Cut each Camembert wheel into four equal portions, wrap each portion in plastic wrap and freeze for 1 hour.

2 Place flour, mustard, mixed herbs and black pepper to taste in a small bowl and mix to combine. Place bread crumbs and chili powder on a plate and mix to combine. Roll each Camembert portion in flour mixture to coat, then dip in egg and roll in bread crumb mixture. Place on a plate lined with plastic wrap and freeze for 15 minutes longer.

3 Heat oil in a large saucepan until a cube of bread dropped in browns in 50 seconds. Cook cheese portions a few at time for 30 seconds or until golden. Remove, using a slotted spoon, and drain on paper towels.

4 To make sauce, place cornstarch and water in a small saucepan and mix to combine. Stir in blueberries, sugar, nutmeg and lemon juice and cook over a medium heat, stirring constantly, for 4-5 minutes or until sauce thickens. Serve sauce warm with fried Camembert.

Serves 6

The secret to frying Camembert is to have it really cold before you start so that the outside cooks and forms a golden crust that hides a barely melting center.

Cheese Sauce

$^{3}/_{4}$ cup/90 g mature Cheddar cheese
2 tablespoons/30 g butter
2 tablespoons all-purpose flour
1 cup/250 mL milk
$^{1}/_{2}$ teaspoon dry mustard
3-4 drops hot red pepper seasoning
$^{1}/_{4}$ cup/60 mL dry sherry
freshly ground black pepper

1 Shred cheese and set aside. Melt butter in a heavy-based saucepan, stir in flour and cook over a medium heat, stirring constantly, for 1 minute or until mixture is bubbly.

2 Using a wire whisk gradually whisk milk into flour mixture and cook, stirring constantly, to make a creamy sauce. Stir in mustard, pepper seasoning, sherry and black pepper to taste and cook, stirring constantly, until sauce boils and thickens.

3 Add cheese to sauce and stir until cheese melts. Remove sauce from heat and serve immediately.

Makes $1^{1}/_{2}$ cups/375 mL

The secret to making a good cheese sauce is to add the cheese right at the end of the cooking time. After the cheese is added, very little additional cooking is required as the heat of the sauce melts the cheese almost immediately. If the sauce is heated for too long after the cheese is added the cheese will become tough and stringy.
If making the sauce in advance, add the cheese after reheating the sauce.

Feta Cheese Pastries

3 eggs, lightly beaten
3 tablespoons chopped fresh parsley
freshly ground black pepper
1 lb/500 g feta cheese, crumbled
8 sheets fillo (phyllo) pastry
1/2 cup/1 stick/125 g butter, melted

1 Place eggs, parsley and black pepper to taste in a bowl and whisk to combine. Stir in cheese and mix well.

2 Take 1 sheet of pastry and cut in half. Brush each half with melted butter and fold each piece in half. Place a spoonful of cheese mixture in the center of each piece.

3 Bring pastry up around the filling and squeeze to resemble a bag. Brush with butter and place on a lightly greased baking sheet. Repeat with remaining pastry and cheese mixture. Bake pastries for 20-25 minutes or until golden. Serve immediately.

Makes 16

Oven temperature
400°F, 200°C

When using fillo (phyllo) pastry keep the pastry not being used covered with damp paper towels or a clean damp cloth. This prevents the pastry from drying out and cracking.

For a better shape, you might like to cook these pastries in lightly greased muffin cups.

The Perfect Omelet

There are many different omelets, but the one that seems to hold the greatest mystery is the traditional 2-egg, meal-in-a-jiffy, plain French omelet. Once you have mastered it, you will wonder what all the fuss was about.

PREPARING THE OMELET

Place the eggs, water and seasonings in a bowl and lightly whisk to combine. Allow 1 teaspoon of cold water for each egg used – this makes for a light omelet.

COOKING THE OMELET

Start by melting a knob of butter in the pan over a medium heat and tilt the pan to ensure that the entire surface is covered. When melted, the butter will foam and then subside. This is the time to pour in the eggs. Wait a few seconds to allow a thin film of egg to form on the bottom of the pan and, using a fork or spatula, gently draw in the sides of the omelet, allowing the uncooked liquid to flow onto the pan surface. Continue in this way until the omelet is cooked.

The best omelets are made with 2 or 3 eggs for a single serve. As the cooking time is short, the omelet will not overcook and toughen.

THE COOKED OMELET

This should be only lightly set, with the top still moist. Once cooked, fold over one-third of the omelet away from the handle of pan. Hold pan over a warm serving plate, with the palm of your hand uppermost. Shake omelet to edge of pan and tip to make another fold and slip onto serving plate. If preferred, the omelet can be folded in half. The cooked omelet can be sprinkled with a filling before folding. Always serve an omelet immediately it is cooked.

Bean Sprout Omelet

1 teaspoon butter
2 eggs
2 teaspoons water
freshly ground black pepper

BEAN SPROUT FILLING
2 tablespoons/30 g butter
2 teaspoons grated fresh ginger
4 tablespoons bean sprouts
1 tablespoon snipped fresh chives

1 To make filling, melt butter in a small skillet and cook ginger, bean sprouts and chives for 1 minute. Remove pan from heat and keep warm.

2 Melt butter in a small omelet pan. Lightly whisk together eggs, water and black pepper to taste. Pour into heated pan and cook over a medium heat. Continually draw edge of omelet in with a fork during cooking until no liquid remains and omelet is lightly set.

3 Sprinkle the bean sprout mixture over omelet and fold. Slip onto a plate and serve immediately.

Serves 1

Bean Sprout Omelet

RATATOUILLE CREPES

Oven temperature
350°F, 180°C

1/2 cup/30 g fresh bread crumbs
1 cup/125 g shredded mature Cheddar cheese

CREPES
1 cup/125 g all-purpose flour, sifted
2 eggs
1 1/4 cups/315 mL milk
1 tablespoon/15 g butter, melted

RATATOUILLE FILLING
1 eggplant, cut into 3/4 in/2 cm cubes
2 tablespoons olive oil
1 onion, chopped
14 oz/440 g canned tomatoes, undrained and mashed
1 teaspoon dried oregano

To keep cooked crêpes warm while making the rest of the batch, place the crêpes in a stack on a heatproof plate and place in a low oven, or over a saucepan of simmering water.

1 To make crêpes, place flour in a bowl and make a well in the center. Add eggs and a little milk and beat, working in all the flour. Beat in butter and remaining milk.

2 Pour 2-3 tablespoons batter into a lightly greased 7 in/18 cm crêpe pan and tilt pan so batter covers base thinly and evenly. Cook over a high heat for 1 minute or until lightly browned on base.

To freeze crêpes, stack cold crêpes between sheets of waxed paper or freezer wrap and place in a sealed freezer bag, or wrap tightly in aluminum foil. To use crêpes, thaw at room temperature, then fill and reheat. To use directly from frozen, remove waxed or freezer wrap, stack 4-6 crêpes, wrap in foil and heat in oven at 400°F/200°C for 25 minutes.

3 Turn crêpe, using a spatula or palette knife, and cook second side for 30 seconds. Remove from pan and set aside. Repeat with remaining mixture.

4 To make filling, place eggplant in a colander, set over a bowl, sprinkle with salt and allow to stand for 30 minutes. Rinse under cold water and pat dry with paper towels. Heat oil in a large skillet and cook onion over a medium heat for 4-5 minutes or until soft. Add eggplant, tomatoes and oregano and bring to the boil, then reduce heat and simmer, uncovered, for 15-20 minutes or until mixture reduces and thickens. Remove pan from heat and set aside to cool.

5 Divide filling between crêpes and roll up. Place crêpes in a single layer in a shallow ovenproof dish. Place bread crumbs and cheese in a bowl, mix to combine, sprinkle over crêpes and bake for 30 minutes.

Serves 4

Ratatouille Crêpes

Smoked Salmon Quiches

Oven temperature
400°F, 200°C

2 sheets prerolled frozen puff pastry, thawed

SMOKED SALMON FILLING
6 eggs
$1^1/2$ cups/375 mL whipping cream
$^1/4$ teaspoon ground nutmeg
freshly ground black pepper
4 oz/125 g smoked salmon, chopped
2 teaspoons chopped fresh dill weed

3 Divide salmon mixture between pastry shells and bake for 10-15 minutes or until quiches are puffed and golden.

1 Cut out twenty-four pastry rounds using a $2^1/2$ in/6 cm cutter. Press rounds into shallow, greased small muffin pans or tartlet pans.

2 To make filling, place eggs, cream, nutmeg and black pepper to taste in a bowl and whisk to combine. Mix in salmon and dill weed.

Makes 24

These quiches can be made in advance, removed from the pans and stored in a covered container in the refrigerator. To reheat, place quiches on baking sheets lined with nonstick parchment paper and heat at 400°F/200°C for 5 minutes or until quiches are heated through.

'Smoked salmon should be pink-orange in color, moist and with a mild smoky smell and delicate flavor.'

Smoked Salmon Quiches

Useful Information

In this book, ingredients such as fish and meat are given in ounces so you know how much to buy. It is handy to have:

- A small inexpensive set of kitchen scales.

Other ingredients in our recipes are given in tablespoons and cups, so you will need:

- A nest of measuring cups (1 cup, 1/2 cup, 1/3 cup and 1/4 cup).
- A set of measuring spoons (1 tablespoon, 1 teaspoon, 1/2 teaspoon and 1/4 teaspoon).
- A transparent graduated measuring cup (4 cups or 1 cup) for measuring liquids.
- Cup and spoon measures are level.

QUICK CONVERTER

US Standard	Metric
1/4 in	5 mm
1/2 in	1 cm
3/4 in	2 cm
1 in	2.5 cm
2 in	5 cm
4 in	10 cm
6 in	15 cm
8 in	20 cm
9 in	23 cm
10 in	25 cm
12 in	30 cm

MEASURING LIQUIDS

US Standard	Cup	Metric
1 fl oz		30 mL
2 fl oz	1/4 cup	60 mL
3 fl oz		90 mL
4 fl oz	1/2 cup	125 mL
5 fl oz		155 mL
5 1/2 fl oz	2/3 cup	170 mL
6 fl oz		185 mL
7 fl oz		220 mL
8 fl oz	1 cup	250 mL
16 fl oz	2 cups	500 mL
20 fl oz		600 mL
24 fl oz	3 cups	750 mL
32 fl oz	4 cups	1 liter

METRIC SPOONS

US Standard	Metric
1/4 teaspoon	1.25 mL
1/2 teaspoon	2.5 mL
1 teaspoon	5 mL
1 tablespoon	20 mL

MEASURING DRY INGREDIENTS

US Standard	Metric
1/2 oz	15 g
1 oz	30 g
2 oz	60 g
3 oz	90 g
4 oz	125 g
5 oz	155 g
6 oz	185 g
7 oz	220 g
8 oz	250 g
9 oz	280 g
10 oz	315 g
12 oz	375 g
13 oz	410 g
14 oz	440 g
15 oz	470 g
16 oz (1 lb)	500 g
1 lb 8 oz	750 g
2 lb	1 kg
3 lb	1.5 kg

OVEN TEMPERATURES

°F	°C
250	120
275	140
300	150
325	160
350	180
375	190
400	200
425	220
475	240
500	250

INDEX